Sketch & Paint Techniques

ANIMALS & WILDLIFE

JEAN PARRY-WILLIAMS · MARTIN KNOWELDEN

DIAMOND BOOKS

This edition published 1995 by Diamond Books
77–85 Fulham Palace Road
Hammersmith, London W6 8JB

First published as two volumes:

Learn to Paint Animals © Jean Parry-Williams 1983, 1986
Designed and edited by Youé and Spooner Limited

Learn to Paint Wildlife © Ruan Martin Ltd 1985, 1986
New edition 1986
Design and photography by Rupert Brown

ISBN 0 261 66541 3

Printed in Italy

CONTENTS

ANIMALS
Jean Parry-Williams

PORTRAIT OF AN ARTIST
JEAN PARRY-WILLIAMS

Jean Parry-Williams was brought up in the country and lived in a home which was always full of animals. Her house was situated on the Cheshire-Derbyshire borders and so she was well placed to visit all the fine galleries and museums in and around Manchester. This, coupled with the encouragement of her father who took her from an early age to see paintings whenever possible, has made her one of the lucky ones. She says of herself, 'although perhaps not born with a silver spoon in my mouth, I was certainly blessed with a pencil in my hand.'

In the 1930s Jean Parry-Williams won several children's drawing competitions, run by the *Manchester Guardian*, with scenes of animals set in local surround-

ings. During her school days she took Honours in all the Royal Drawing Society examinations and won a special prize for drawing animals. Also during this time she exhibited in the National Children's Academy in London run by the *Sunday Mirror*. After leaving school she studied at the Royal Salford College of Art and then spent a year in Vienna at a well-known studio and was thrilled to have the chance of studying from the portfolios of original drawings by Albrecht Dürer. Here, too, she was lucky enough to attend and sketch the rehearsals of the famous Lipizzaner horses in the Spanish Riding School.

Jean has exhibited in various provincial and London

The steeplechaser *High Clouds* 41 × 51cm (16 × 20in)

open exhibitions, including the Royal Academy, and has had her own shows of mixed-media paintings held in London. These shows also toured the provinces. However, animal portraiture began to take up more and more of her time as commissions started to come her way. When she lived in Hampshire, the local paper, the *Southern Evening Echo*, commissioned her to write and illustrate several articles after seeing some of her work done during an annual sketching visit to Crufts Dog Show. Later, on moving to Gloucestershire, *Cotswold Life* magazine also published several articles with animals as the central theme. Jean writes and illustrates articles for the *Leisure Painter* and regularly

gives lectures and demonstrations for Daler-Rowney. In addition, she works as a freelance lecturer for various Colleges of Further Education and is the tutor for the Cheltenham Tutorial College Pastel Course. She also runs small painting classes from her own studio in Painswick, Gloucestershire.

Although Jean Parry-Williams specializes in animal portraiture and has appeared on television demonstrating this, her favourite subject, she also enjoys painting landscapes, seascapes, still life and portraits in oil, watercolour and pastel. Her paintings are in many private collections throughout the United Kingdom and as far afield as Denmark, Pakistan and the USA.

WHY PAINT ANIMALS?

There are many reasons! You may want to have a record of a favourite dog or cat and a quick sketch or finished drawing would be just the thing. Or perhaps you want to be more ambitious and paint an oil, watercolour or pastel portrait to hang on your wall as a reminder of a beloved pet who is no longer with you. Or you may just love animals and want to portray some of their beauty and character in a drawing or painting. Photographs seem to lack some of the vitality of a drawing or painting and although animal portraiture poses many problems, you may feel you want to take up the challenge and try to capture on paper or canvas some of the personality, mood, expression and even humour of an animal. I hope I can help you do this.

How often, when painting a landscape, have you felt that animals placed here and there would just complete the picture? Perhaps your scene is a Welsh or Scottish hillside, with sheep in the distance. Maybe you are painting a view of meadows with cattle steadily munching among the grasses, or lying contentedly chewing the cud. Sometimes, a group of horses make a colourful picture grazing in their paddock or standing alert watching some distant object. In each case, if you are not sure of their basic shapes you will probably leave them out, wishing all the time that you were more confident and able to paint them.

Animals have a natural grace and rhythm which you may long to capture in a picture. Even when still they have a pent-up force which can be released in a moment; this is the essence of most animals. Even a sleeping dog or cat is always on guard. There is the speed of a galloping horse

with its flowing mane and tail; the ripple of underlying muscles and the bone structure of a fleet-footed grey-hound; and even cows, calves and pigs can have sudden surges of movement.

These to me are all very good reasons for wanting to learn to paint animals and I hope I can help you gain the confidence to do just that.

Keeping a Scrapbook
I find it very useful to keep a scrapbook of newspaper and magazine cuttings of animals. It provides an invaluable source of reference material if there is no model immediately available and you want to check a position or a point of anatomy. It can also spark off ideas and give you inspiration when you have one of those blank periods. Be methodical with your collection and keep different animals together, i.e. dogs in one place, cats in another. I don't stick down my cuttings but keep them loose in their sections so that I can easily take them out for reference. This also facilitates increasing or discarding parts of the collection. Specialist animal books which often have anatomical details can be helpful but you can't beat the real thing. Work from nature as much as you can, in every possible situation.

Choosing a Subject
When you set out to draw or paint an animal you must choose your subject carefully, especially if you are a beginner. Unlike human models you cannot rely on your animal model staying in the same position for very long (unless, of course, it is asleep). I always try and train my own dogs to sit still for long periods. In fact, a dog to me is more than a special member of the household, it is my assistant and model at many painting demonstrations. Ideally, one's subject should have good proportions and features, well-defined muscle and bone structure and an intelligent, attractive face. It is also much easier to draw and paint an animal who has a kind and docile nature. But if you are painting someone else's animal you will obviously have to get used to the animal possibly being nervous, irritable and moving around a lot. On such an occasion it is useful to make quick outline sketches, not only to familiarize yourself with the animal, but so that you have several different positions to choose from.

On the opposite page you can study three paintings of my puppy, Tess. A lot of careful thought and many sketches of different poses preceded these (see also pages 46–47). I cannot stress enough the need to make preliminary sketches and to draw, many times, every animal you want to paint.

USING
A SKETCHBOOK

LIKE ALL ANIMALS, DUCKS KEEP ON THE MOVE
SO KEEP THE LINES FLOWING.
THESE ARE WHITE AYLESBURYS.

BROKEN EDGES TO OUTLINES GIVES FLUFFY
EFFECT

TAWNY OWL
I HAVE SIMPLIFIED
THE PLUMAGE INTO
ESSENTIAL SHAPES
AND MARKINGS.

Your sketchbook should be your constant companion and guide. It will gradually become full of notes, thumbnail sketches, plans and even finished drawings. Try and carry a small one with you wherever you go and practise drawing at every opportunity – while waiting for the bus, sitting in the park or shopping at the market. Draw anything and everything as it is only by constant practice and observation that you will perfect your drawing. You can sketch while watching television even though a single picture is seldom held for more than a few seconds. Naturally, you should take a sketchbook to any events where there are likely to be animals, for example, the racecourse, local dog shows and country fairs. Make studies of animals at the zoo or at the circus – these places are a great source of information and inspiration.

A sketchbook is a very personal thing because it records an artist's thoughts and ideas as they are forming. It is invaluable to supplement sketches done as preludes to painting with written notes, as you will see from the pages of my sketchbook reproduced here. These notes can be general comments about the animal, its character and personality, or swatches of colour to help you remember the colours accurately when you are back in the studio.

Let me explain here what I mean by a sketch and a drawing. To me, a sketch is a quick, rough impression of a subject caught in a few lines, either in black and white or in colour, whereas a drawing is a detailed study of a subject using all kinds of different mediums. This detailed study can be the preliminary stage before you start the final painting, or it can be a finished drawing in its own right that you may well want to frame and hang on the wall. I always do several careful drawings (as well as preliminary sketches) of an animal before I actually paint it and you will see some of these drawings and sketches on the next few pages.

NOTICE HOW CLOSE EARS ARE TOGETHER, AND HOW LARGE WITH HEAD AND BODY SIZE

SHOWING BUILD UP FROM BASIC GUIDELINES

11

DRAWING AND
SKETCHING MATERIALS

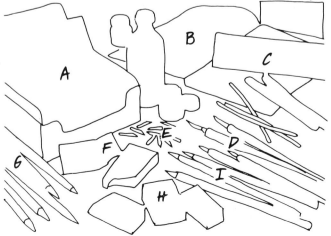

A DRAWING INKS
B SKETCH-PAD
C WILLOW CHARCOAL
D DRAWING PENS
E PEN POINTS
F KNEADABLE PUTTY RUBBER
G BALLPOINT, FELT-TIP PENS
H ERASERS
I PENCILS

I use a great variety of tools to gain the effects that I want when sketching and drawing and you can see some of these in the picture opposite. Throughout the text these and the uses to which I put them are described in some detail but here I am concerned with a general list. Hard and soft degrees of pencils from HB to 6B (the latter is the softest grade) are obvious choices but I also use ballpoint and felt-tip pens, sticks of charcoal and charcoal pencils, Conté crayons and pastels. Conté crayons come in white, black, sanguine (copper coloured) and grey. Throughout this book the pastels I refer to are Artists' Quality Soft Pastels. Students' Quality Pastels are invariably much harder. Fountain pens, Rotring pens, old-fashioned dip pens and indian ink (with a bottle of water so that you can dilute its strength), a kneadable putty rubber and fixative are also essential for most people. Above all do not forget a sketch-pad. I generally use an A3 landscape sketch-pad of white cartridge paper 297 × 420mm ($11\frac{3}{4} \times 16\frac{1}{2}$in).

The drawings of the Jack Russell Terrier were done in ballpoint pen, heightened with Conté crayon and coloured pencils. While doing these drawings I sat on a sofa in his owner's flat drinking coffee, with a biscuit meant for me given in small bits to the little dog to keep his interest. It is often necessary to have little titbits handy. As he moved from one position to another I sketched each one. He had a way of sitting up begging for minutes at a time, crossing one paw over the other and comfortably leaning back on his stumpy tail with his back to the fire. Once he almost dropped off to sleep sitting there bolt upright! Of course you must never laugh at animals. Their feelings are very easily hurt and once their confidence in you is lost it is very difficult to regain it. Dogs usually keep still better than cats but this cat in my pencil drawing was very helpful. While I was working on sketches for a painting of two dogs, he stalked into the room and watched the proceedings from a suitable vantage point on the back of an armchair. I suddenly became aware of his intense stare. The opportunity was too good to miss, so using a 3B pencil I started to draw him. I quickly sketched in the general body shape and then blocked in the dark areas with cross-hatched lines. Next, I drew the shape of his head, ears, and his eyes. I then worked on the other details and finished by paying attention to his hair markings.

This poodle, however, was a very different type of subject. He had an intense black coat and a cheeky temperament! For my first sketch I used a black medium-tip ballpoint pen. He was finally painted in pastel with the mid-tones of his tight curls in Cool Grey Tint 4 and the highlights on them executed with touches of white Conté, while Burnt Umber Tint 4 was ideal for his dark brown eyes.

Jean Parry-Williams.

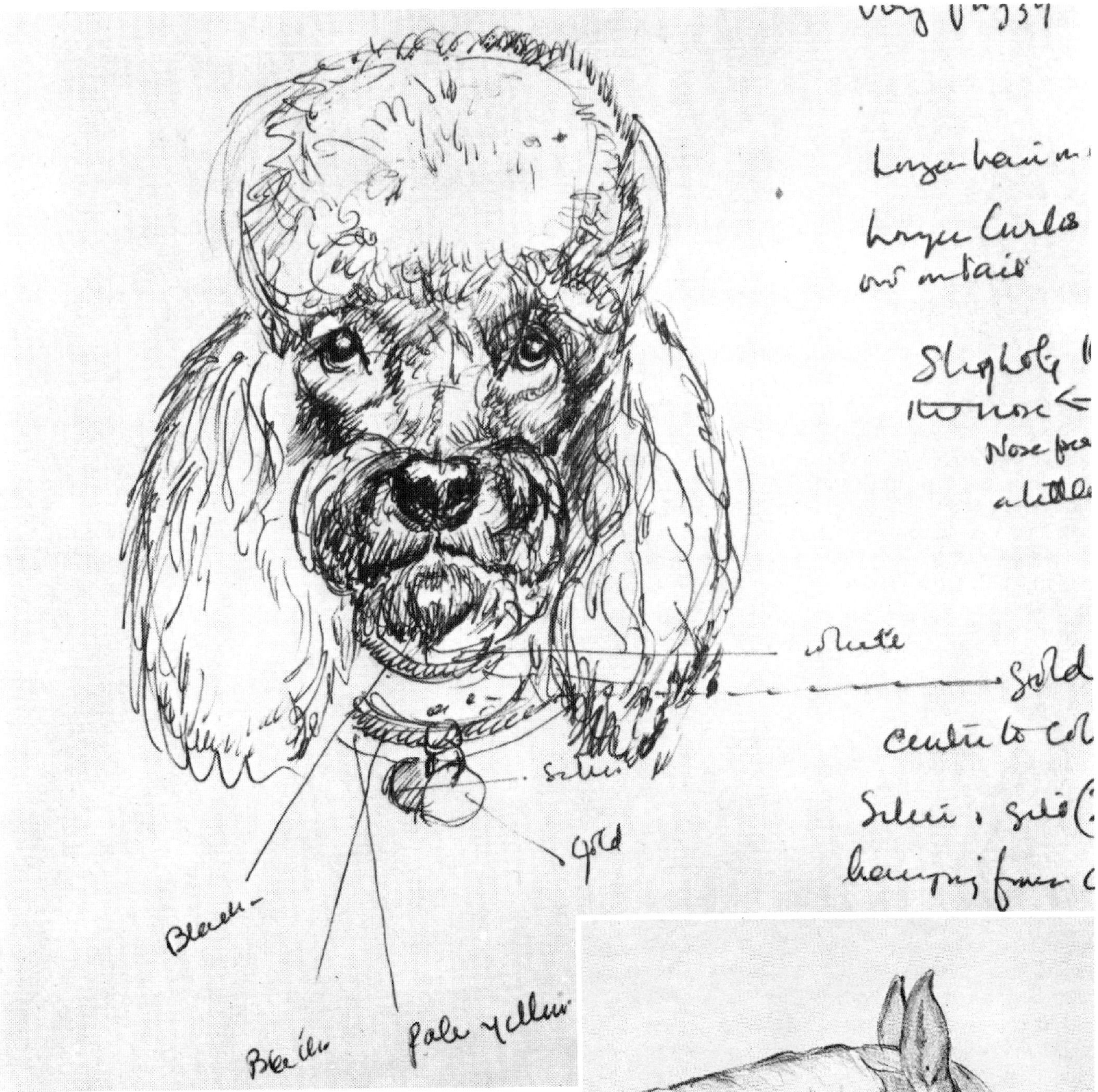

During one of my animal painting courses, the horse shown here dozed in the warm afternoon sunshine. As my students drew and painted him from various angles, I did a quick sketch of his head. I used a stick of willow charcoal to outline the head shape. For the colours of his neck and head I used the pastels Yellow Ochre Tint 4 with Autumn Brown Tint 3 for the lighter, and Burnt Umber Tint 4 for the darker, tones on his mane. The pink round the muzzle was lightly indicated with Burnt Umber Tint 2 with a touch of Rose Madder Tint 0.

15

SHAPE AND PROPORTION

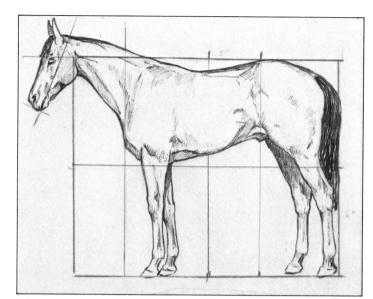

Fig. 1

It is natural for you to want to start work on your final painting as quickly as possible, but you should not rush ahead so fast that you make avoidable mistakes in the drawing stage which are then difficult to put right once you start painting. Once again, I must stress the importance of sketching and drawing. With practice and continuous observation of animals you will become more proficient and will soon be able to avoid the more obvious mistakes in shape, proportion and anatomy. However, until you reach that stage of proficiency, there are a few simple devices which you can include in your preliminary sketches to help you to observe accurately.

All artists have their own method of working. Some base their drawings on stick figures, some on egg shapes or blocks. For my own use I have devised a combination of ideas which may help you to work out the proportions which are so important when drawing animals. Ideally, you should study the anatomy: the skeleton, the shapes of the joints and the limit of their movement, and then look at the underlying muscles. Next, look closely at the animal and see how the skin lies over the muscles and the way the hair grows.

Basic Framework

When you begin to draw an animal a basic framework is helpful. You will find it best to draw an outline of the animal on this framework before you proceed to the smaller details. With experience you will be aware of the relationship between the larger shapes and be able to see the proportions clearly. We will take as an example a 'standard' horse but you can apply these principles to any other animal. Remember that although I say a 'standard' horse, all animals are individuals and vary considerably.

Fig. 1 shows the side view of the standard horse fitted into a basic framework. The horizontal and perpendicular lines help you to sort out the proportion.

Compare the size and proportions of the heavy Suffolk Punch (**fig. 2**) with the standard horse.

Fig. 3 shows how the front view of a horse's head fits into a 'coffin' shape and how it is equally divided by a perpendicular, central line. The two angles on either side of the top of the 'coffin' show where the ears fit and where the eyes are placed – approximately a quarter of the way down the face on the outer edges of the head. It is useful to choose the head, a prominent feature, as a yardstick against which you can measure other parts of the body.

Fig. 2

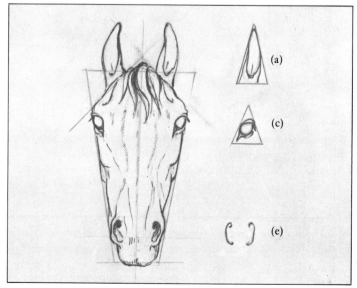

Fig. 3

16

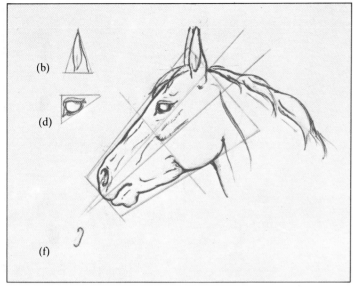

(b)

(d)

(f)

Fig. 4

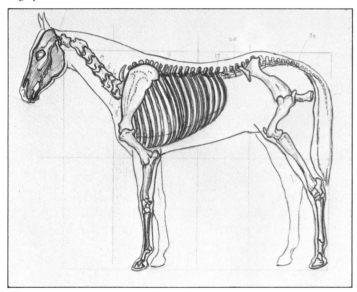

Fig. 5

If you slant the 'coffin' shape (**fig. 4**) and draw the head within it you will notice how much of the face comes above the central line and how the approximate positions of the various features compare one with another.

In **fig. 5** we can see how the skeleton fits within the outline of the horse. If you study this it is obvious that certain areas of the body are shaped by the underlying bone structure.

In **fig. 6** we see the head again full on. The bones of the skull and its moulding make it clear how the structure of the head is made up.

There are certain 'shorthand' shapes within which parts of the horse's body can be drawn. Look at the full face and side view of the head and you will see how the ears fit into a tall narrow triangle (**a** and **b**). The eye in each case will roughly fit into a triangle (**c** and **d**). Note the eyelashes grow out at an angle, not straight out sideways. Full face, the nostrils are like two commas facing in towards each other (**e** and **f**). From the side, the hooves are a triangle (**g**) but viewed from the front they are a curved wedge-shape (**h**). Depending on how far the ear is swivelled forward, you may or may not see inside it (see **figs. 1** and **4**).

You will find that once you have got the respective sizes and angles right and in proportion, the other details of the animal's anatomy will follow more easily.

Another useful tip is to place an old cardboard mount of a suitable size over the picture you are working on (**fig. 7**). This makes a temporary frame through which to work and helps you to bring the whole image into the right scale and proportion. Alternatively, you can use two right-angled pieces of card which can be overlapped to form the correct image area and to show the effect of a coloured mount surrounding the painting.

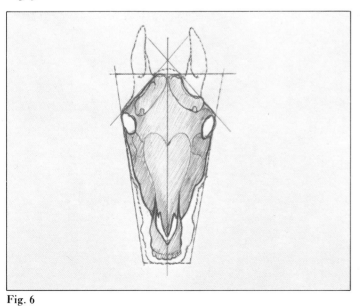

Fig. 6

Fig. 7

17

ANATOMY AND FORESHORTENING

Anatomy

When you have had some practice in drawing a particular animal, you will begin to get a feel for its anatomy and will be able to judge whether a particular pose is possible or not. Do not forget to consult your animal anatomy books and remember that photographs can help enormously at this stage. Obviously, there is not the space to go into detail here about anatomy and indeed it is a complicated subject which would fill a whole book, but often it can help to run your hands through the fur of an animal to feel the structure beneath – for example, how the legs bend. This is especially helpful when the length of an animal's fur tends to obscure the details of its anatomy. You can see this in my portrait of the little white dog in oils on pages 41–43.

Beware of one common anatomical mistake: the legs of an animal – so often the beginner gets their anatomy wrong. The joint at roughly the mid-point of the hind legs is the ankle and not, as one might expect, the knee. Consequently, it does not bend in the way a knee would; it bends backwards. Of course, with the front legs, the knees bend in the same way as human knees.

In my colour sketch of the resting greyhound, you can see the muscle and bone formation – the leg tendons are especially noticeable. I often find it helpful to compare my own bone structure with that of the animal I'm drawing. The animal kingdom has the same skeleton and skull formation as humans, but various areas differ in proportion

e.g. the neck of a giraffe is very much longer than that of a human! Also, some joints are positioned differently e.g. the knee and elbow joints in a horse and a human being.

Foreshortening

Foreshortening takes place when a shape is turned at such an angle to you that what you see appears elongated or shortened, or you see something exaggerated as in the 'front-on' views of the St Bernard and the horse illustrated on page 19.

If you look at **figs. 8** and **9**, you will see that viewed from the front, the body of the horse is compressed into the shape of an upright barrel – or should I say, several barrels, receding away from you. It is always useful to draw two vertical guidelines when doing this kind of foreshortened view of an animal, as you will find it easier to work within such a framework. The shoulders and chest of the horse are then compressed into a second barrel-shape and then back on the furthest plane you see the curve of the belly and top of the hindquarters.

In my sketches of the greyhound, which are good examples of foreshortening, the distance from nose-tip to shoulder appears greater than from the shoulder to the tail. This is a considerable exaggeration since in a straightforward profile the shoulder-tail distance would be the greater.

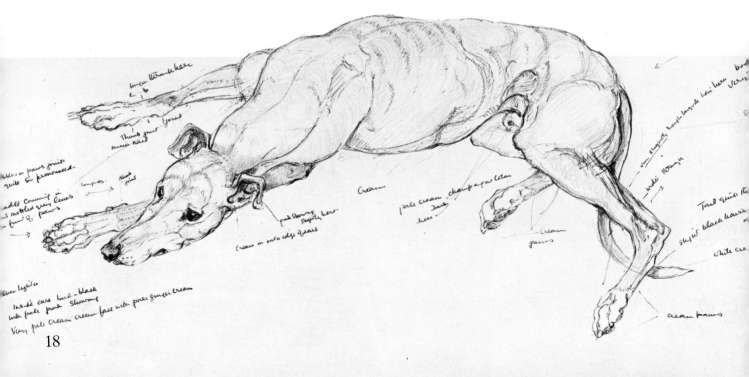

The head of the St Bernard is very large in comparison to his body. On the left his front leg sticks out at an awkward angle and seems too long.

Judging the degree of foreshortening is always difficult because if it is overdone your painting will look distorted. Once again practice and careful observation are the answer.

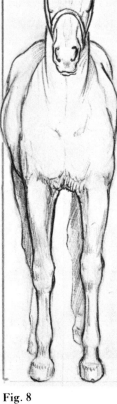

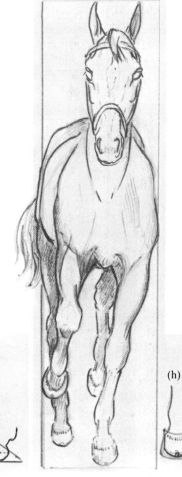

(g)

(h)

Fig. 8   Fig. 9

USING PASTELS AND CHARCOAL

Pastels

Pastel drawing can be said to have originated in prehistoric times when early cavemen drew animals and hunters on cave walls, using coloured earths. Some of these fascinating paintings, often up to two metres high, can be seen in the caves of France and Spain, the most famous being at Lascaux in S.W. France. Modern pastels are made by adding to the pigment an inert substance such as china clay to control their strength. Artists' Quality Soft Pastels range in tint strength from o, when a large quantity of clay is added, to 8, which contains a large amount of pigment, and hence is a much stronger colour. Soft pastels are one of the most stable mediums that an artist can use and are highly regarded by professionals. Artists' Quality pastels are called 'soft' because this describes their character (a few are hard in certain colours at their greatest strength). There are varieties of cheap pastels which are hard and difficult to use because they are scratchy and so I do not recommend them. Artists' Quality Soft Pastels have their tint number on the wrapper together with their name. An extensive range of colours and tint strengths are available.

I break my pastel sticks into short lengths, using the sharp broken edge for line work and the side for thick sweeps of colour where I need to fill a large area with solid colour. Personally, I find pastel one of the best mediums for painting animals as it is especially good for portraying hair and fur such as the dense quality of a heavy-coated large dog like an Old English Sheepdog; the soft fur of a cat or the smooth satin-like texture of the glossy coat of a well-groomed horse. A great variety of colours are obtainable and these can be mixed either by placing tints in short strokes side by side, or by painting dots of different colour very close together, as did some of the French Impressionist painters like Seurat. One pastel can also be lightly imposed over another to make yet another colour. You can blend the colours together by rubbing them in with a stump of finely rolled paper, or your fingers. You can fix the pastel and work on top of it; in short you can use it in a great variety of ways.

Oil Pastels

Oil pastels are made by mixing the pigment with an oil and wax. They were invented by a Frenchman in the nineteenth century but have only become available comparatively recently for general use. The best are available in a large number of tints. They are compatible with oil paints and can be blended with turpentine to produce a wash effect. They should not be used in conjunction with Artists' Quality Soft Pastels. They are particularly useful for quick sketching on the spot.

Paper

As with the pastels themselves, there are a large variety of papers to choose from. They come in different weights, colours and textures, but it is advisable to have a paper which is tough enough to stand erasing and with enough roughness or 'tooth' to hold amounts of pastel loaded on to it. If the paper is too thin it will show tiny creases and may tear when you are rubbing out. Colours vary and you will obviously choose those which will give a suitable background for the type of picture you are painting. For most animal work I generally use a pale fawny-beige pastel paper, but with black or white animals a stone coloured or grey-toned pastel paper is better. Some artists use a white watercolour paper which they tint with a suitable colour wash.

Charcoal

Charcoal is made from the thin peeled twigs of the lime or willow which are heated to glowing point, without the free access of air, until they are completely carbonized. Lime and willow woods are best as they are free of resin and give a rich colour. Any wood containing resin, such as fir or pine, produces a vegetable tar which, when carbonized, would smear if used for drawing.

Boxes of charcoal sticks can be purchased from most art supply stockists. These sticks are rather fragile to handle, but pleasing in richness and depth of tone. They can be broken and used in short lengths. It is not necessary to sharpen them as the broken end can be used to give a sharply defined line. The sides of the broken short lengths can also be used to add shadow and texture. The sticks come in various thicknesses, from thin to thick, the thickest are called 'scene painters charcoal' in England.

Charcoal is also made into pencils. The charcoal is compressed and inserted into wooden sheaths in the same way that a lead pencil is made. The charcoal pencil does not break as easily as the stick of charcoal and it can be sharpened to a point. Such charcoal pencils are available in various strengths from hard to soft in a similar way to an ordinary lead pencil. Charcoal may be used on any paper suitable for pastel painting.

If you wish to lift out a single mistake a kneadable putty

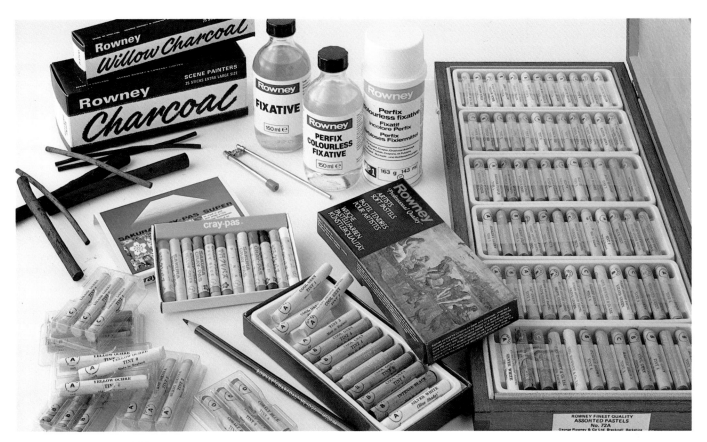

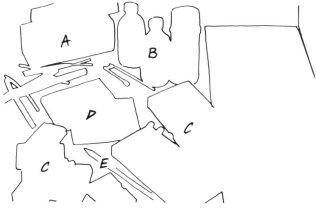

A CHARCOAL
B FIXATIVES & SPRAY DIFFUSER
C ARTISTS' QUALITY SOFT PASTELS
D OIL PASTELS
E CHARCOAL PENCIL

rubber is best. If a large area is wrong, use a clean cotton rag – smack the paper with the rag or rub it over the surface. One tip which may be useful if you should have to erase and find you have mislaid your putty rubber – the soft inside of new bread works wonders! But do be careful not to include the butter if you are eating sandwiches out of doors. I have still not discovered how to get rid of grease marks on paper!

Fixative

If you wish to protect your pastel and charcoal work against smudging, you should consider preserving it under glass or using a fixative – or both. Charcoal spray fixatives contain a shellac to coat the drawing and stop the particles of charcoal moving or becoming smudged. For pastels, a PVA-based resin in aerosol form is preferable. However, all fixatives do, very slightly, dull the colours. When using an aerosol fixative always spray in a well-ventilated space, preferably out of doors.

Although I use more pastels than those mentioned in this book, I suggest that beginners start with a basic palette of the colours listed below:

Ivory Black	White (Cream Shade)
Cool Grey Tint 4	Cobalt Blue Tint 6
Prussian Blue Tint 1	Yellow Ochre Tint 4
Sap Green Tint 5, 8	Lizard Green Tint 3
Autumn Brown Tint 3	Burnt Sienna Tint 2
Burnt Umber Tint 6	
Black charcoal pencils	Black charcoal sticks,
Conté crayons: black,	thick and thin
grey, white, sanguine	

USING OILS

Oil painting became popular in the sixteenth and seventeenth centuries, although pigments had first been mixed with an oil binder several centuries earlier. Today sunflower, poppy and linseed oils are the main binding agents mixed with pigments.

Artists' Quality Oil Colours are the best available. Beginners, for whom price might be a consideration, should use Rowney Georgian Oil Colours.

With oils, colours do not run into each other as they can with watercolours. So, different colours can be applied next to each other or on top of each other and they will not mix unless worked in with a brush. As the paint remains malleable for several hours, it is encouraging for the beginner to know that any mistakes can be wiped away with a rag, or painted over.

Basic Equipment for the Beginner

1. A set of good quality oil paints (see page 23). Some suggested colours for your basic palette: Titanium White, Ivory Black, Cobalt Blue, Viridian, Lemon Yellow, Naples Yellow, Yellow Ochre, Cadmium Yellow Deep, Burnt Umber, Burnt Sienna, Crimson Alizarin (or Indian Red). I always use Crimson Alizarin but it is a very strong colour and should be used sparingly. If you find it too strong you could use Indian Red instead. With these colours you can mix all the colours needed for most pictures. There is, however, an enormous range of oil paints from which to choose if you do wish to expand your palette later.
2. A box to hold your paints.
3. A palette on which to arrange and mix your paints (see page 23).
4. A palette knife for mixing your colours and to scrape off unwanted paint.
5. One bottle of pure turpentine and one of linseed oil.
6. A double dipper (or two single ones). One dipper holds your thinning medium which can be either turpentine or turpentine mixed with linseed oil, depending on the stage you have reached in your painting. The other dipper is to hold turpentine for cleaning your brushes whilst painting.
7. A sturdy, folding easel which will take reasonably large as well as small canvases and can be used either indoors or outdoors.
8. A lightweight stool if you want to sit down while working.
9. Paint rags or kitchen roll on which to wipe brushes.
10. A selection of brushes. Brushes come in many shapes and sizes and traditionally the most popular are sable hair and hog bristle brushes. There are also brushes made of man-made fibres, such as nylon, available (see below).
11. Stretched canvas or canvas boards on which to paint (see below).

Always buy the best equipment you can afford. If you look after it, it will last for years. This particularly applies to brushes.

When buying canvas or canvas board, it is important to decide upon the texture of canvas surface you want to paint on as it will have a great bearing on the work you produce. For delicate and detailed work, choose a medium or smooth-grained canvas, but if you want a feeling of vigour and strength a rough surface will help give this effect. As prepared canvas on stretchers is very expensive, you can buy canvas on rolls and cut it to the required size, and then put it on stretchers yourself. For everyday work I use canvas boards 51 × 41cm (20 × 16in).

The following brushes would make a good basic stock: Flat Hog Bristle Series 120 No. 4 for early drawing in on canvas, Series 125 No. 12 to fill in backgrounds and Series 123 No. 6 for other work. I also use Nylon brushes Series 220 Nos. 2, 4, 5, 6, 8 and 10. If this series is unavailable Series 233 will do. I find a Sable brush Series 133 No. 4 ideal for painting small details such as eyes, whiskers, etc. It is also useful to have several large No. 6 brushes either Hog Bristle Series 123 or Nylon Series 220 so that you can use a different brush for each colour mix.

Brushes should be rinsed in turpentine or white spirit after use and then washed with soap and water until completely clean. Finally, they should be drawn back into shape between fingers and thumb and left to dry, standing upright in a jar.

Palettes are made in various shapes and sizes. The most common shapes are oval or rectangular. They can be made of wood, plastic, metal or greaseproof paper. I prefer wood. When you have finished painting for the day, scrape off any surplus paint with your knife. Some paint may be hardly used so put it in an airtight container for future use. Then wipe the surface of the palette with a rag dampened with turpentine. It is always best to start with a clean palette, so that when you next want to mix colours they will be clear without old colours showing through.

I always use a palette knife for mixing my paints because if you use your brush the various colours will build up in the ferrule (where the bristles are attached to the base of the handle) and may transfer unwanted colour on to your painting.

Before you start to paint, it is sometimes advisable to tone down the colour of the white canvas as it can be very dazzling, especially out of doors. You can do this by moistening a rag with turpentine which has been mixed with a little dark colour, such as Burnt Umber, and rubbing this

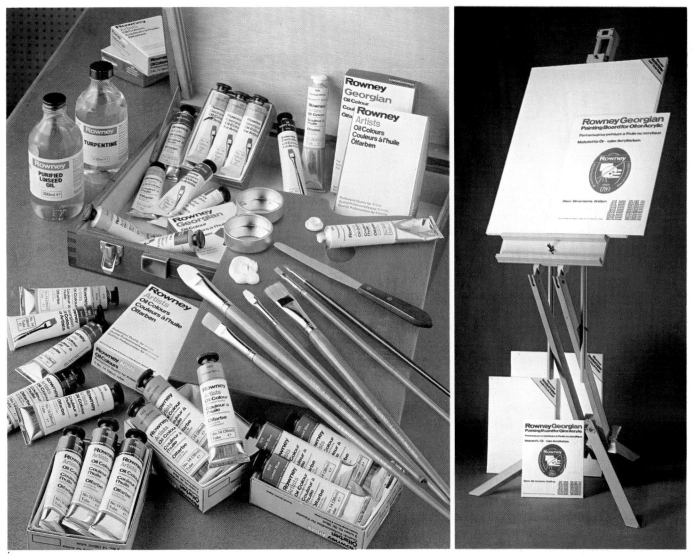

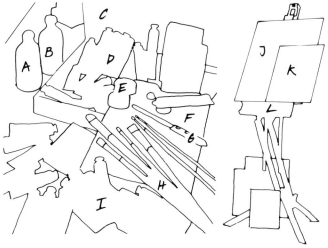

A LINSEED OIL
B TURPENTINE
C PAINT BOX
D GEORGIAN
   OIL COLOURS
E DIPPERS
F PALETTE
G PALETTE KNIFE

H BRUSHES
I ARTISTS'
   OIL COLOURS
J STRETCHED
   CANVAS
K PAINTING BOARD
L EASEL

mixture evenly over the surface of the canvas. When this is dry I make the initial sketch of the subject using a No. 4 brush and Burnt Umber thinned with turpentine. Then I take a rag dipped in this mixture and block in the large shapes and darkest darks. I am then ready to start the actual painting.

Paint can be applied thickly (*impasto*) or thinly, depending on the effect you want. The most usual method is to start with thinly applied colour and build up as the picture progresses, commonly known as 'lean to fat'. This is technically the best way to work but remember that light colours are improved by painting thickly, dark colours are not. Don't be afraid to load your brush with colour and paint it on to the canvas with firm strokes. Some of the pleasures of using oils are the rich texture, the depth of tone you can achieve and the quality of brush strokes.

USING WATERCOLOURS

Watercolour is finely-ground pigment, bound with gum arabic that is soluble in water. It is available in solid or cake form, as well as in tubes. The tubes of Artists' Quality Watercolours have glycerine added to keep them moist. Students' Quality Watercolours are also available.

Watercolour is transparent and when placed on white paper, the paper will show through. This imparts a brightness to the colours that cannot be obtained in other mediums, except perhaps coloured inks. The inexperienced tend to think that watercolour is an easy medium to use, perhaps because they were taught to paint at school with poster colour. Certainly watercolour is convenient to use as you can easily carry around a small box of watercolours with a sketchbook, pencils, some brushes and a small flask of water. However, you need a lot of practice and experience to master watercolour painting and although it is an exciting and exhilarating medium, it can also be very difficult and frustrating!

Whatever subject you choose to paint in watercolour you must give it a lot of thought and planning before you actually start to paint. Sort out your ideas in advance and do several preliminary pencil sketches. Work out where the darks and lights in your picture will fall. Then decide on the correct colour and try to make do with one wash rather than two or more. When you mix up your washes on your palette take care to think of the hue, tone and relative temperature of each colour, red is a hot colour, blue is cold. Spontaneity is part of the charm of watercolour so don't overwork your painting. Also, leave the background impressionistic. Work in broad washes and don't try to put in too much detail – but do treat the main subject with more emphasis than the rest of the painting.

Paints

Your paintbox should have a palette attached to it, usually this forms the lid of the box. The best are made of tin with a white enamelled surface; moulded plastic boxes are also available but these tend to discolour quite easily. Cheaper boxes have paints already in them but with the better ones it is possible to choose your own paints. The colours are in tubes, whole pans and half pans and you will need Artists' Moist Watercolours. When you are starting out I suggest you just buy the following colours: Cadmium Yellow, Burnt Umber, Ivory Black, Cobalt Blue and Crimson Alizarin and add to your palette as you progress.

Brushes

A good selection of brushes to start with would be: Round Sable Series 34 Nos. 6 and 8. If these sable brushes are well cared for they will last a lifetime, but as sables are expensive I can recommend instead Round White Nylon Series 270 Nos. 4, 8, and 12 and Round Mixed Hair Series 60 Nos. 4, 8 and 12.

I manage with only three brushes. One sable: I prefer a No. 6 size (or its equivalent in the excellent nylon brushes) a larger brush of squirrel, badger, or a mixture of hairs (or again nylon) for washes, and a smaller No. 2 or 3 nylon brush for finer details. When choosing a sable brush, test first to see if the bristles will form a point when damp. Ask if you may dip it into clean water, then wipe it and flick off the excess water. If it is a good brush the tip will come to a fine point.

Easels

An easel is useful, especially if you wish to stand when working, and there are a variety to choose from. Buy a sturdy folding one which will double for working outside as well as inside.

Watercolour Paper

This comes in sketchbooks, block pads, or in various sizes of loose sheets. If you use loose sheets of paper, they will have to be mounted on a drawing board either with drawing pins, clips or gummed tape. Watercolour papers come in three surfaces: Rough, Not and Hot Pressed. For the beginner, Not, which has less roughness or 'tooth' is the easiest paper to use as it is neither too thin nor too thick in texture. Paper is also sold by weight. Choose about 300gm² (120-140lb) weight of paper for loose sheets as this heavy paper is firmer and will not cockle so easily.

Stretching Paper

The best way to prevent cockling is to stretch your paper. Take your sheet of paper and completely immerse it in clean water. I use the bath, as you don't want to bend a sheet by pushing it around in a small area such as a basin or sink. When thoroughly wet, hold up the paper by the corner to drain off the excess water. Now place the sheet flat on a wooden drawing board which is slightly larger than the sheet. From a roll of gummed paper-tape cut four lengths which will overlap both the paper and the board. I use a small damp sponge to thoroughly moisten each length of gummed strip which I then place along the edge of each side of the paper in turn, overlapping on to the board. Press down gently but firmly and leave flat overnight to dry naturally. Do not dry it artificially with a heater. Next morning the paper will have shrunk tight and be ready to use.

Methods of Watercolour Painting

Practise making large and small washes of watercolour on your paper. Angle your sketch block or mounted paper

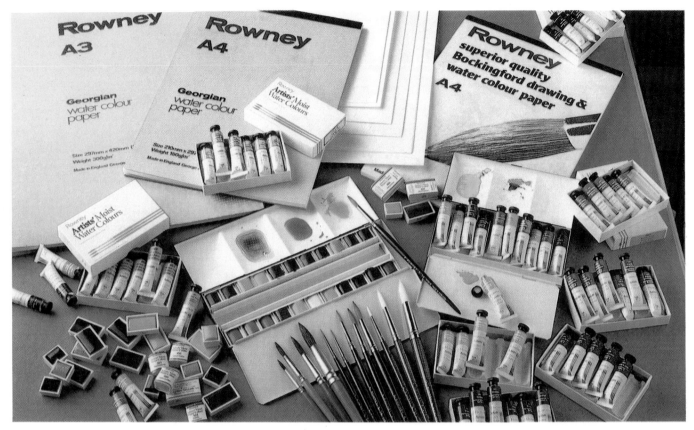

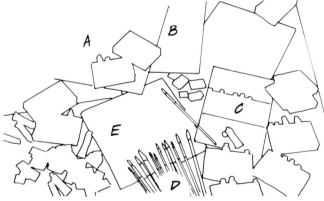

A WATERCOLOUR PADS
B WATERCOLOUR PAPER
C TUBES OF ARTISTS' QUALITY WATERCOLOURS
D SABLE, NYLON, MIXED HAIR BRUSHES
E PANS OF ARTISTS' MOIST WATERCOLOURS

slightly towards you so that the wash will flow downwards easily. Dampen the paper first with clean water, and then with a brushful of colour already mixed in your palette, start at the top left-hand corner and work across and down the paper until the area you want to paint with the wash is completely filled. If necessary, replenish your brush as you go. If you mix a generous quantity of colour in the palette there should not be any change of colour and in this way you can ensure an even wash. If you want a darker tone of the same colour, another wash painted over the first will give a richer shade. This can be done while the first wash is still wet. For a graded wash of colour, add more clean water to the mix in your palette so that the colour will become paler when added to the wash already on your paper. It is best not to add white to watercolours to create lighter shades. Instead, add more water and in this way you can retain the brightness of the original colour. White paint tends to make the colour appear cloudy and less pure.

If pure white is wanted on your picture leave this area unpainted, letting the paper show through, or carefully lift the colour out with a sponge or tissue while the paint is still wet. As I said, a watercolour can be made darker by going over it a second time, but once on your paper it is not so easy to make it lighter. It is here that you can avoid mistakes by thinking ahead.

The 'wet-into-wet' technique of adding more wet paint into an already wet area of paint on the paper to run together the colours and tones, is a difficult method to control. However, it is highly effective for creating atmosphere in skies, distance, horizon and portraying mist or rain and is, therefore, worth practising. For the dry brush technique, fill your brush with colour, wipe or blot off the excess water on a tissue or blotting paper and then drag the brush across the area to be painted so that a broken, stippled effect is created. This is a useful method for painting dappling on horses, or a mane or tail flying in the wind.

EXERCISE ONE
CALVES
IN CHARCOAL

Having just discussed the different uses and potential of the four mediums I generally work in, it will be helpful to describe specific exercises executed in each of these four mediums.

Near my house is a lovely Cotswold farm which was originally, a wool mill powered by the Painswick Brook. Apart from its fascinating stone buildings and beautiful rural setting, the farm provides a seemingly unending supply of charming calves from its fine herd of cattle. The kind owners allow me to sketch and take my students there to draw and paint whenever I like, and the enchanting calves make wonderful models. As soon as possible they are weaned from their mothers and taken into the byres where they have warmth and protection on straw-covered floors with plenty of room to move about. Some of the buildings are divided with partitions to make smaller areas and in these you find a few calves huddled together. For the artist these conditions are ideal, as the animals cannot move very far and you can lean against the walled partitions or sit on a straw bale under cover and in relative comfort with your sketchbook.

Calves are easily startled, so when you are painting them don't make sudden movements. Being very inquisitive animals, when they are used to you being there, they will soon come crowding up to try to lick the charcoal or nibble the edge of the sketchbook. The light in the byre is often dim, but there are subtle tones in the walls, straw, timbered low roof, and the wooden partitions between the stalls. On a summer's day, the sunlight shafts through causing shimmering here and there. The colours of the calves make contrasting patterns in this setting.

One of the first things that strike you when starting to draw or paint calves is their solid and compact forms. Their bodies lack sharp corners or straight lines and everything about them seems to softly curve. The only things which are fairly straight are their long eyelashes, not curling up as one might imagine but jutting out at an angle. Their little cloven hooves are generally pale cream or grey and gently rounded. When drawing calves you will find that their shape and proportion are quite easy to see if you conform to certain basic rules (see also pages 16–17 on Shape and Proportion). Here are a few guidelines which may be of help to you.

With each of the calves shown on these pages, you will notice that the body, legs and head fit into an elongated egg shape. But the head, when seen full on, is the shape of a diamond, with the top and base flattened. The ears come out at right angles from either side of the flattened top. Being only babies, the heads are larger in proportion to the rest of their bodies than those of cows. The measurement down the length of the ear is slightly less than the width between the eyes. The width of the muzzle fits roughly twice across the space between the eyes. Measuring down the head, from the top of the poll to the base of the muzzle, the length of the ear will fit about two and a quarter times. Naturally this varies with the angle of the ears, and depends on whether they are bent forward or back. You will see that they jut out sideways, and do not stand up like those of a horse or donkey. This also applies to sheep, goats and deer. Notice, too, that the eyes are set on the outer edges of the skull, and the nostrils, like two inverted commas, face into each other near the outer edges of the nose.

Try to vary the positions of the animals you draw and paint. It would be dull to have them all in similar attitudes or poses if you were making a group. Of course, if they are in a byre they will spend a lot of time standing together, and if there is hay in the manger they will face towards it. Delightful groupings can be made when the calves are standing with wisps of hay being chewed and pulled from

the heap. They also spend a lot of time with their backs towards you and this position will require you to take into account foreshortening, as the head will look smaller from this angle (see pages 18–19).

I used charcoal for all these drawings of the calves. You can use ordinary willow charcoal in sticks or charcoal pencils. If you should want to rub out, use a kneadable putty rubber. Unless it is vital to remove a wrong line I generally leave it. Extra lines often give character to a sketch. I find a sketchbook of white cartridge paper best for charcoal work. Although it may seem wasteful, it is advisable to use only one side of the paper when using a sketchbook. If you don't have a spray fixative with you then your drawings are less likely to smudge if there is a plain sheet of paper on top of them when you have to close the sketchbook. Do try and fix your charcoal and pastel drawings as soon as you get home.

EXERCISE TWO
PIGS
IN PASTEL

It must have been the hottest day of the year when I decided to make the preliminary sketches of the pigs illustrated here. It had taken me weeks to find a farmer who had a sow who had just farrowed. Piglets are most appealing when they are very small, so I had to try and sketch them only a few days after they were born.

With my largest sketchbook in hand, and a selection of charcoal, loose pastels and Conté crayons, I set off for the farm on the kind invitation of the owner. Even five days after the piglets' birth it was still necessary to be very quiet as there was the danger that the mother might take fright and lie on them. The shed was stiflingly hot because the heaters were constantly on to protect the piglets from draughts. Baby animals need enclosed spaces which are warm and dimly lit, so at first it was not easy to see the piglets snoozing in a heap in the straw after a satisfying meal from mum, but gradually my eyes adjusted to the light. Fortunately, I had taken the precaution of wearing my oldest clothes and a head covering. In the heat the strong smell of the shed and its inmates permeated everything. I could even taste it!

The edge of the stall was of a handy height on which to lean my sketchbook and, with a charcoal stick rather than a charcoal pencil, I started to sketch the general shape of the group of piglets. Speed was essential because, although

they seemed to be asleep, every time I looked up from my drawing one of them had moved! Here there was advantage in numbers as a position was generally duplicated by another piglet. Once I'd sketched in the basic form of the group, I then started to concentrate on individual piglets. Each had its own personality. One, a bit larger than the others, found a comfortable place on its mother's back while the little runt of the litter sat disconsolately against the sow's foreleg while brothers and sisters snuggled comfortably in a heap against her hindquarters and body.

I made a separate drawing of the sow. The texture of her skin with its long white hairs emphasized the strength of the great muscular body. The ears had a shell-like quality of folds and curves, and little veins showed through in places. The nose ended with several wrinkles, and the front of it, where the nostrils were, was like a movable disc which swivelled back and forth as she sniffed the hot air.

Composition

It is one thing to make sketches, but quite another to sort out from those preliminary sketches a suitable combination and arrange them to make a pleasing composition for a finished picture. Scattered drawings, however good, have little impact in a painting unless a good deal of thought has gone into grouping them to make a unified whole. For

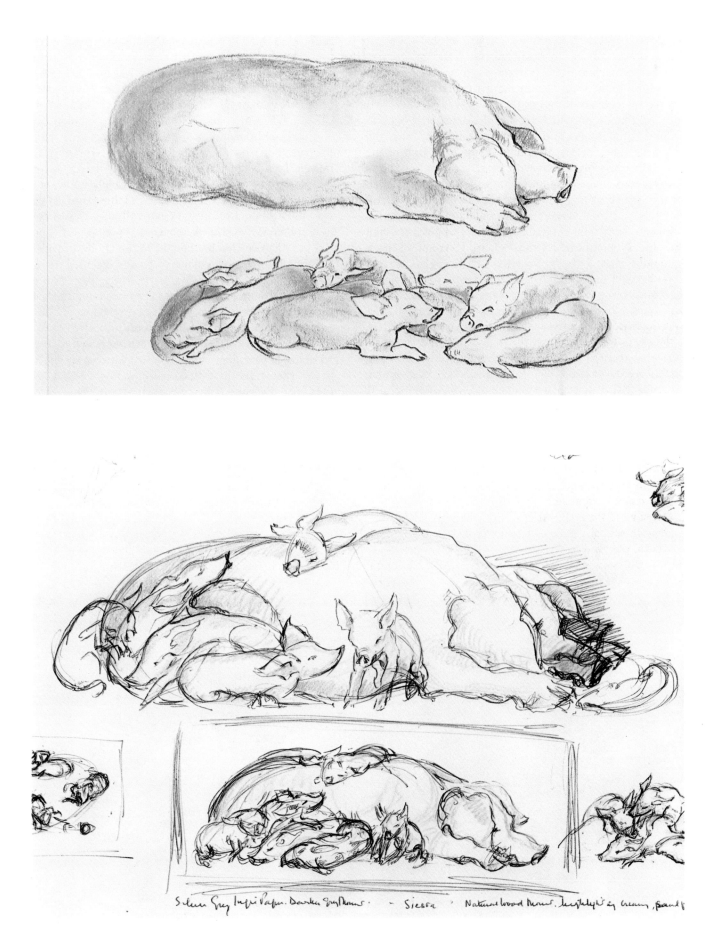

Silver Grey Ingres Paper. Darker Greytones. — Siesta. Natural wood floor. Highlights in cream, pearl.

example, if this group consists solely of curved shapes it will look too soft so, to break this, at least one upright angular form should be introduced to give impact to the composition. With this in mind I experimented with several different groupings of the piglets against the sow's body but finally put the largest piglet across her back to break that long curve and lead the eye down towards the group of piglets below. I thought of the little runt of the litter. His upright position with his straight little forelegs pushing back against the sow's side was just what I needed for my angular shape. As you can see from the sketches on these pages, I tried various arrangements and ideas before I arrived at my final choice. This is very important when planning a complicated painting and I cannot stress it enough. I altered the positioning of the piglets several times before I was satisfied. The drawing of the sow across the top with the group of piglets beneath (on page 29) was the sketch I originally drew on location in the shed. The drawing was outlined in charcoal and partially filled in with sanguine Conté.

In the close-up of the runt of the litter (this page) you can see how he is placed against the sow's side. Notice how he is slightly knock-kneed and, when drowsy, his eyes became elongated slits. When small, piglets' ears are erect so you can see the detail of the inside formation. The nose

is not so pronounced as in an adult, and the head seems far too big for the body. Most babies, whether humans or animals, often give this impression but here it is exaggerated by the foreshortening of his position. Notice, too, the little cloven hooves. All these features are important and you should train yourself to be observant of such details.

I used white Conté to indicate the long white hairs on the sow and for the underlying thick skin over heavy muscle I used the side of a 12mm (½in) length of broken pastel, Rose Madder Tint 0. The darker areas were done with Burnt Sienna Tint 2; sanguine Conté was used for the very dark tones; and the darkest of all were drawn in with delicate strokes of soft black charcoal pencil.

I gave a great deal of thought to the choice of paper: its weight, texture and colour. I finally decided to use a medium-weight stone-coloured Ingres paper. The tones of the sow and piglets showed up well on this colour background. Remember to think in advance about your background colour as it is important.

Before starting, I padded my drawing board with about 10 sheets of newspaper to make a soft backing for the pastel paper, then carefully pinned it to the board with drawing pins, making sure that it was quite taut. You could, of course, use any kind of scrap paper for backing. Next, with a 6B pencil I very lightly drew in the whole composition

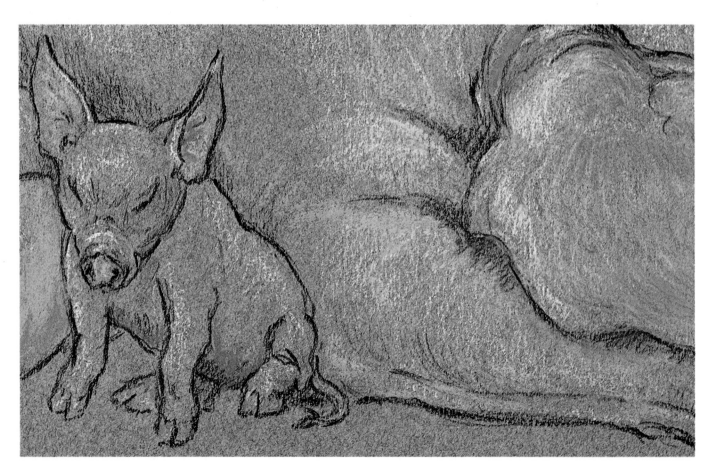

that I had decided upon in my preliminary sketches. Only when I was quite sure that the drawing was correct did I move on to the next stage. With a finely sharpened black charcoal pencil I lightly drew over the pencil outline. Any mistakes at this stage could have been taken out with a putty rubber by gently lifting off the wrong line. I find this method of going over a faint pencil outline more satisfactory than using a tracing which is apt to lose something of the original drawing.

Where a shadow was cast, say under the sow's foreleg and ear, or where it overlapped the shoulder and front leg, I darkened the line by giving more pressure to the stroke. Where light fell on an upper surface, like the top of the piglets' backs or the sow's ear, I used less pressure and this produced a fainter line.

The next stage was to fill in the shape of the animals. I broke a white Conté to about 12mm ($\frac{1}{2}$in) and using the side of it broadly swept in the shape of the sow's body with curves following the shape of the general form and the underlying muscles. I emphasized with white Conté where the light caught the upper surfaces: a wrinkle on her nose, the upper curve of the nearside ear and down its flap and the top of the hindquarters. I did the same thing with the piglets. Then I used the black charcoal pencil, and with

very fine lines drew in the shadows beneath the sow's ears where the ears stand away from the head, and also where the group of piglets were leaning against her side. Next, I added some colour with sanguine Conté under and on the surfaces of the sow's ears. Here the tiny red veins were lightly detailed with the same colour Conté. The sanguine Conté was also used in the darker coloured areas on the piglets. Inside the ears of the runt, under his tummy, and any places which needed a deeper colour I used Burnt Sienna Tint 2 pastel in strokes following the body contours. I used Rose Madder Tint 0 for the lightest colour tones and the basic stone-coloured paper was left uncovered to provide the mid-dark tones. I worked over the whole picture in this way and then stood back to make a final check. I added a highlight here and a touch of dark there until I was satisfied I could take the picture no further.

All that remained was to sign it and hand it over to my framer. I then had the pleasure of seeing it hung in The Pastel Society's Annual Exhibition at The Mall Galleries in London.

EXERCISE THREE
ALSATIAN
IN OILS

I have organized this exercise so that, if you would like to, you can follow it step-by-step. But do read through the whole exercise before you start.

If you look at the first sketch of Cass the Alsatian (**fig. 10**), you will notice that he looks rather disgruntled and cross. In fact he was bored! As his owners did not want him to look like this, alterations had to be made before I did the final drawing on to the canvas for the portrait. To make him look more alert I made the ears prick up and brought them closer together. I also raised the upper eyelids, thus giving him a kinder expression and brought his tail closer to his hindquarters so that his thick hair was shown to advantage. In fact I made his whole pose more

alert. This kind of thing is hard to do when you are a beginner and it takes years of practice but if you study **figs. 10** and **15** carefully you will see how I have altered his expression.

I chose a medium-grained canvas paper size 76 × 51cm (30 × 20in) and, to make it easier to achieve the correct proportions for the dog, I divided the canvas into rectangles by drawing a horizontal and a perpendicular line at the centre of the picture. I went on to make further equal divisions (**fig. 11**). With a more complicated subject I would have made more divisions on the canvas. The central horizontal and perpendicular lines divide the dog's body in half, with the ears, forehead, shoulders, rib cage and top

Fig. 10

of the hindquarters above the central horizontal line, while the lower part of the head, the eyes, stomach and lower quarters and tail come below this line. Check with **fig. 10** and you will see what I mean.

It is a simple matter now to draw the different parts of the dog in these boxes and thus keep everything in proportion. Drawing a boxed framework like this also helps you to keep a space at either side and above and below the dog. It is very important to have the subject placed correctly on the canvas.

If you like, you can sketch out the initial drawing lightly on to the canvas with a stick of willow charcoal, sweeping off any mistakes you may make with a clean brush, rag or tissue. I did my painting straight off with a No. 5 flat hog bristle brush using Burnt Umber diluted with turpentine. This makes the paint thinner and so it flows more easily and can be wiped off in case of error. Remember, if you sketch out your first drawing with charcoal you will have to go over it again with Burnt Umber to fix it.

The colours I used for **fig. 12** were arranged on my mixing palette from left to right: Ivory Black, Cobalt Blue, Viridian, Yellow Ochre, Naples Yellow and a large squeeze of Titanium White. (White is used in the mixing of most colour tones so you will need plenty.) Then Cadmium Yellow Deep, Burnt Umber and Crimson Alizarin. This is quite a restricted palette but from these basic colours you can mix all the tones necessary for painting animals. I find that it always helps to arrange the colours on your palette in the same order every time to prevent confusion.

You will also need a medium to thin the paints which makes them easier to work. Generally this is a mixture of equal parts of turpentine and linseed oil. Keep this in one half of your double dipper (do not overfill it). In the other half you should have turpentine for cleaning your brushes. I always use a palette knife rather than a brush to mix my paints.

Having drawn in the initial outline of the dog with Burnt Umber you will then need to strengthen this outline with Ivory Black before going on to the next phase, which is blocking in the shapes of the dog's markings. Study **fig. 12** carefully, and then proceed. The markings on the Alsatian are black, so, with a No. 6 flat nylon brush and a mix of Ivory Black and turpentine lightly paint in the dark areas. Where grey is needed, for instance on the ears, shoulders and highlights on the nose and rib cage, add White to the Black mix. We now move on to the pale brown and cream areas. Mix Naples Yellow and White on your palette and then, with a clean brush, thinly paint in all the pale brown parts of the dog. Add more White to this mixture for the cream areas. For the deepest tones on the hindquarters, hind legs and tail root, use Naples Yellow undiluted. Apply the same colour, but thinned with turpentine, on the dark areas of the head, ears, shoulders and elbow. For greater impact, place a thin mix of Black between the front and hind legs and along the base of the stomach. Then with the same colour carefully draw in the nose. Notice that this

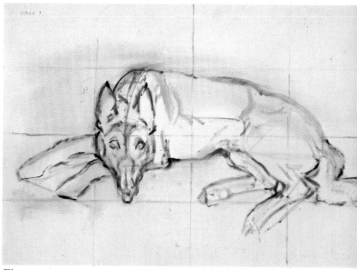

Fig. 11

Fig. 12

Fig. 13

Fig. 14

work over the background as advised. If you look at **fig. 13** you will see that the background is lighter in tone at the extremities but darker where the dog is lying as this helps to indicate shadow. For these darker tones add more Burnt Umber and a little Ivory Black to the original background mix.

Going back to the dog itself you need to fill in some more colour and details. When painting the inside of the ears add more White, a touch of Crimson Alizarin and Burnt Umber to make a soft pink. Darken the outer edges of the ears with Ivory Black, blending down into the grey of the ear.

Great care is needed to paint the eyes so I will take you through this in detail, for the whole liveliness of the picture depends on their expression.

Carefully examine the detail of the face in **fig. 14**. Using a Rowney No. 6 Sable brush Series 133 moistened in medium and with Ivory Black, draw in the upper lid and down the inner side of the eye outlining the tear duct and the slightly dark area below it. Then paint the outer edges of the eye and the shadow area leading up towards the outer base of the ear. Then draw in the shape of the eyeball, but notice that the top is shadowed by the upper eyelid. Next paint the pupil and fill it in. With a similar clean brush, place a dab of White at the top of the eyeball as the highlight, dragging the brush downwards leaving a slightly jagged edge where it blends into the dark area of the pupil. Using another clean brush, paint in the rich brown of the eyeball. For this mix use Burnt Umber with a little Cadmium Yellow Deep and a touch of Crimson Alizarin. Moisten your brush and paint in one curve. Add a little more Cadmium Yellow Deep and lightly touch the brown where the light reflects on the eyeball. Check with **fig. 14** again. Using the same colour but slightly diluted with medium, paint the smooth hairy area round the eye and down into the inner corner against the top of the bridge of the nose. Repeat this method to paint the other eye. Lastly, paint the curve of the eyebrow whisker follicle above each eye. Now you have reached the final stage of putting the finishing touches to your painting (see **fig. 15**). I was fortunate in having a live model, but I hope the stages we have gone through together have been helpful. Compare them carefully with my finished painting and you will see if there is much more to do to your own picture. The background has still to be completed and you do this using the same colour mixes, brushes and method as earlier in the painting. Use the same short strokes working methodically over the whole area, so that no canvas is left uncovered. This is really an abstract background, made up of most of the colours used to paint the dog so that there is harmony in the painting.

You will notice in my final painting that I have softened the edges of the dog's colours and markings. To paint in the rougher areas of the dog's coat you must apply the paint with thick sweeping strokes following the direction of hair growth. This *impasto* treatment is also used for the

is foreshortened, so that the nostrils show only as two small dots. Draw a thinner mix of Black across the shadowed base of the nose, just allowing the nostrils to show through faintly. Only indicate the outline of the eyes at this stage.

The background must now be filled in around the dog (see **fig. 13**). This is done with short strokes of the brush always working outwards and away from the animal with quite thick paint. I find this method gives a more sparkling effect than applying a smooth surface of paint.

For the background colour, place White on your palette, add Cobalt Blue and a little Viridian, then Yellow Ochre and Burnt Umber and mix it all together with your palette knife. The medium for moistening the brush from now onwards should be equal parts of turpentine and linseed oil. The linseed oil adds a richness to the paint. If you continue to use only turpentine as a medium in the later stages of the painting the paint will end up looking too thin and dried out.

The brush I chose for the background was No. 6 Rowney filbert-shaped Nylon Series 220. With the above mix,

Fig. 15

ruff of hair on either side of the face and the thick tail hair.

For highlights on the coat, for example on the rib cage, a smoother appearance is needed and you achieve this by using more medium in the mixture so the paint blends evenly on the surface area. Check the direction of the light source and strengthen the resulting shadows by darkening the existing colours. In my painting this occurs on the right side of the head, on the elbow, tail and on the hind legs. Use a darker tone of the same colours originally mixed for these areas. Paint in the paw pads with grey for their highlights toning down to the darkest shadows with Ivory Black.

Small details, such as toe-nails, need careful attention. Using a No. 6 sable brush, paint the pale cream on the soft paw pads and then the grey, made as before from White with Black added, which subtly changes tone to rich black in the deepest shadows. For the toe-nails use a pale cream (made by mixing White and a little Naples Yellow) and dark Burnt Umber, toning to black underneath. When you put the finishing touches to the muzzle, use a thin blend of

Naples Yellow and White, toned down with Burnt Umber. Finally paint in the nose, toning the highlight of grey with a little Ivory Black. I always find that it is good to leave the finished painting for at least a few hours and then come back and look at it carefully. You will be able to observe any little unfinished details much more clearly after a break, and I do hope you are pleased with your finished painting.

Fig. 16

Fig. 17

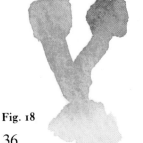

CADMIUM INDIAN PAYNE'S BURNT
YELLOW RED GREY UMBER

Fig. 18

EXERCISE FOUR
CAT
IN WATERCOLOUR

The preliminary drawing (**fig. 16**) of Soapy the cat was made on Saunders rough surface paper with an HB pencil. As you can see, this is a complete drawing in itself with details of his markings. However, I later decided to carry this drawing further and make it into a watercolour painting because the cat's colouring was so attractive. This is where it is so useful to take colour notes when sketching. Even if you want the drawing to be complete in itself, you never know when you might want to make a painting of such a drawing.

Only four colours were used in this painting as I wanted to keep it simple and no more were needed to portray Soapy's colours. I used Payne's Grey, Burnt Umber, Cadmium Yellow, and Indian Red; and two brushes, Rowney Nylon Series 270 Nos. 8 and 12. You can see how these four colours were mixed in the simple colour chart in **fig. 18**.

To paint **fig. 17** I used a No. 12 brush and made a generous mix of Payne's Grey and Burnt Umber on my palette with plenty of water. I painted a dark wash of this along the cat's shoulder and down between the curled paw and the side of the left ear. Then I took it up over the back and down over the hindquarters and along the outer side of the tail as far as the cat's muzzle. I also used this colour at the top of the neck just behind the head and in-between the ears. When using watercolour in the preliminary stages you must use plenty of water to keep the wash flowing and prevent hard edges forming. Remember to keep your board tilted so that you can control the direction of the wash.

I then changed to a No. 8 brush and made a mix of Cadmium Yellow and Indian Red as shown in the colour chart (**fig. 18**) and I used this wash to paint the pale brown pattern on the body, paws and head. I added more Indian Red to the wet colour and used it for the left cheek, above the eyes, and on the bend of the hind leg. Soapy's pale-brown markings were richer with more yellow along the inner length of his tail so I strengthened these areas with more Cadmium Yellow. Using the tip of the brush and a dip of Indian Red I drew in the outline of the eyeballs, the eyes, the nose and the chin.

For the finished painting (**fig. 19**) I changed back to a No. 12 brush and made another rich mix of Payne's Grey and Burnt Umber and with a well-loaded brush I painted in the dark markings on the body, shoulders and head. Using the tip of the brush and an even richer addition of both colours to the mix, I drew in the ears and then strengthened the dark areas between the ears and forehead

Fig. 19

and along the edge of the bent hind leg.

Next, I made a good rich mix of Cadmium Yellow and Indian Red and ran this into the previous yellow wash along the tail, shoulders and on the bend of the hind leg. I worked more of this rich tone on the forehead adding a little more Cadmium Yellow on the face above the eyes, along the bridge of the nose, inside the ears and into the lighter markings on the tail.

For the background I made a large pool of Payne's Grey and Burnt Umber which I painted all round the outline of the cat. I then made a second wash of the same colours and overlapped the first wash, allowing an edge to form halfway up across either side of the body to differentiate between the background and the area on which the cat is lying. I then ran a third wash from the base of his back and beneath him to just under his paws. When painting abstract backgrounds like this in watercolour you must always use plenty of water and allow each wash to run slightly into the next so that there are no harsh edges and it all blends together harmoniously.

When the background was finished I strengthened the eyes by using another mix of Indian Red and Burnt Umber painted on with the very tip of the brush. The areas around the nose and mouth also needed strengthening in the same way and, finally, I drew the whiskers in very delicately with Payne's Grey and Burnt Umber.

PAINTING HAIR AND FUR

A good animal portrait must incorporate all the different aspects of the animal's appearance to make a finished likeness and therefore painting hair and fur is an important skill to learn. Much of the animal's character and shape will be lost if you do not properly show whether its coat is rough or smooth, long or short or a mixture. Look closely at your subject, and make notes around your preliminary sketches. Look also at the areas where the fur lies in different directions. This is often a clue to the anatomy beneath. If practicable you should gently feel the animal's fur for the muscle and bone structure which it hides. You will then understand the reason why the fur lies as it does.

The effects of light and shadow play an important part in depicting hair and fur. They show whether a coat is glossy or matt and also show the curvature of the body. Generally, shadows form underneath the body and in folds and creases in the hair. The light correspondingly touches the smoother and more exposed surfaces, hence the term 'highlight'.

There are some similarities in the way you should tackle the problems of hair and fur in whichever medium you use. But there are distinct differences too, particularly in painting the undercoat, so we shall look at pastels, watercolours and oils separately.

Pastels

Pastels are very useful and flexible for indicating the different types of hair and fur. You can use the side of the pastel for a light sweep of colour which is suitable for smooth-haired animals (see Siamese cats in pastel on pages 56–59). More pressure will give a denser impression suitable for rougher coats. The sharp edge of a pastel stick can be used to show individual hairs and whiskers.

Choose a colour of paper compatible with the colours of your subject because very often the paper will show through your finished portrait in a few places. This is quite acceptable and indeed, the paper will act as an additional colour in your painting rather than remain a separate background (see the pigs on pages 28–31).

Your first approach should always be to apply just a few colours in broad patches as an undercoat. Where you see one predominant body colour, e.g. reddish-brown, use two similar pastel colours, such as Burnt Sienna and Rose Madder, together in different amounts. This will also impart richness and depth to the undercoat, making it easier to put details in later. These colours should not be too light or too dark. Even at this stage you should make the pastel

Fig. 20 Pen and ink with watercolour on Ingres paper

follow the direction of the fur, lifting the pastel and changing direction as the fur changes on the animal's body. Shadow should be indicated in a slightly darker colour, leaving the strongest darks to be added later.

If the animal's coat is glossy, for example like a horse's, you may wish to add a few broad highlights and then blend each colour in gently with your finger. In this way the colours will not blur completely into each other, but the edges between the colours will be less distinct and more in keeping with a smooth and glossy coat.

Generally, the more shaggy the fur is, the more detail you are likely to put in. You can use a contrasting colour or repeat an earlier colour using greater pressure to show clumps or tufts of hair and draw thin lines for individual hairs. Follow the direction of the hair once again. Do not use too much of your darkest and lightest colours: keep them for real extremes. Draw individual whiskers very finely, especially on the face and head and do not draw in too many.

Watercolours

A successful animal portrait in watercolour should be clear and fresh-looking without too much detail. However, as watercolours are transparent you should try and visualize the successive stages before starting. Mistakes cannot be easily rectified and your first marks will still be visible even when later washes have been applied over them.

Look at the animal you are painting in terms of light and dark. You should always tackle the largest parts first. Mix your colours on your palette with plenty of water – it is better to be too light than too dark at this stage. Leave dry

38

Fig. 21 Watercolour on white Saunders rough paper

any areas that are to remain white, for example the blaze on a horse's forehead. Apply colour in broad sweeps with a fully-loaded sable brush. The brush should be large enough to wash over the animal-shape in one or two passes, but not so large that it cannot be controlled at the edges.

Block in the main areas of shadow in the same way using a darker colour. The undercoat should then be allowed to dry. With slightly thicker paint and using a sable brush, break each area up into a few similar colours and apply these in large sweeping strokes which again follow the lie of the fur and contours of the body. Where necessary these can be blended with a rag, dry brush or your finger. It is important here to capture the variety of colour without making the animal seem like a patchwork of unrelated colours.

Where the fur is smoothest the colour should not be applied too energetically otherwise the shape and detail could be lost. This is especially true on the head and face. Here the small pouches under the eyes and the shape of the muzzle are created by curved brush strokes applied with a sharp, controlled, wrist action. Strong contrasting colours should not be used too freely, but may ultimately be required around the eyes and nose to give them their shape. Use a fine sable brush for this.

If you wish to create the impression of a fairly shaggy, uneven coat you can apply the second wash before the first has dried. This gives a pleasing impressionistic effect rather than an absolutely precise outline. Alternatively, wait until the first wash is dry and then, with the same colour, apply a second wash to those areas which are to be darker. Follow the direction of the fur and the curve of the body. Where the body has received only one wash it will appear glossier because the paper's whiteness is visible through the colour washes. Subsequent stages are done in the same way, but you should not apply too many washes over each other. If you feel that the colour should vary slightly in places, a thin wash of a new, nearly pure colour will be muted when placed over a duller mixture.

Details such as individual whiskers are applied lightly once the washes are dry. A fine sable brush is best for this. Alternatively, a pen dipped in ink of a suitable colour can be used. The colour employed should not contrast too sharply with the wash colour: pure white or black are too strong.

You might find it useful here to compare my two water-colour paintings of Dinky the cat. In **fig. 20** you will see how the cat's outline has been picked out in black pen as well as the nose, ears and eyes. I have tried to portray Dinky's coat and the sleeker fur on her head and paws in contrast to the rest. In **fig. 21** I concentrated on the overall fluffy effect of her dense fur.

Oils

Oil colour as a medium is very well-suited for depicting the texture of fur as it can be put on thickly to give the impression of a third dimension to the painting. Pastel and watercolour, are, by and large, flat and two-dimensional, but oil can be built up layer by layer and streaked and ridged just like the animal's hair itself. I used this technique, called *impasto*, when painting Cass the Alsatian (see pages 32–35).

Initially, you should block in an undercoat in thin paint of approximately the correct fur colour. The paint should be thinned with turpentine at this stage and used with a medium-sized nylon brush (perhaps a No. 4) to draw the animal's outline. The outline should then be filled in by rubbing it with a rag dipped in the diluted colour. Alternatively, a flat-ended hog bristle brush can be used. This first coat should not be applied too smoothly, but should, once again, broadly follow the main directional sweeps of the hair.

Larger highlights on fur should be added in a lighter colour than the main body colour and should be diluted with turpentine. When blended in, these lighter highlights make the coat look smooth and glossy.

But where the coat is rough you will need to apply the paint more thickly. On an animal such as the St Bernard (page 19) several layers of paint may need to be built up. A palette knife can be used quite effectively for this, but you will have more control with a medium-sized hog bristle or nylon brush. Remember to follow the direction of the fur. Paint applied *impasto* in this way can give your portrait real substance and depth with the ridges of *impasto* creating their own subtle shadows.

If necessary, individual hairs can now be overpainted more thinly in a slightly contrasting colour or tone using a fine sable brush. But don't overdo either *impasto* or the finer details.

PAINTING HAIR AND FUR
LITTLE WHITE DOG
IN OILS

For the first sketches of the little white dog I used a black medium-tip ballpoint pen, and wrote notes around the sketch as 'memory joggers' (see **fig. 22**). This little dog was very lively, so I had to work extremely fast. He came to my studio for me to make the first drawings but I thought for the final painting I would prefer him to be sitting on the grass outside. He was very alert and I made some observations of his characteristics. He had one raised 'fly-away' ear, which was white, while the other, which was folded down neatly, was black. Both ears were of a smooth, silky texture, very different from the rough hair over the rest of his body. He had a very shiny little black nose reminiscent of an old-fashioned black, boot button! His nostrils were well defined and his mouth was clear cut but with short hairs falling down across the upper lip. His front legs were slightly knock-kneed and all his toe-nails were neat and well-shaped. The shaggy hair on his body became smoother as it went down his legs to the paws. His tail was held erect and wagged fast and frequently. This look of cheeky alertness was typical of him and I wanted to capture in my painting the feeling that he might jump up at any moment and run off to play.

Before you start any drawing or painting of a shaggy dog, do talk to the owner beforehand and make sure that they will not decide that the dog looks untidy and have its fur trimmed in-between 'sittings'! This has happened to me, and it is most frustrating, as naturally the whole look and expression of the animal is changed. In fact, you have to start all over again.

As I have said earlier in this section it is difficult with rough-coated animals to know what their bone structure is like so you must try to imagine just where the muscles and bones are under all that hair. If you are working from a live model, stroke it gently and you will feel the bone structure beneath. It is very important to look for anything which will help to give you an indication of the body formation. One point to note is that generally the direction of hair growth follows the body shape.

Down the bridge of the little dog's nose there is a definite parting and the hair grows away in opposite directions. It falls in long strands over the cheeks and upper part of the muzzle. The seeming confusion of hair on the top of his head does flow into definite patterns above, around and behind each ear, whereas below the ears, at the back of the head, the nape of the neck and down the shoulders, the hair is slightly shorter. His moustache grows down from either side around his shiny, black nose. Along the centre

of the dog's back there is a distinct parting which runs right down to the tail root. It is important to note all these things about fur and texture when you are doing your preliminary sketches.

For this painting I chose a medium textured canvas board 51 × 41cm (20 × 16in). I used the basic palette as described on pages 22 –23 and the following brushes: Series 220 Nylon Nos. 8 and 6, Series 133 Sable Nos. 6 and 4.

In **fig. 23** I copied the pen sketch from my sketchbook on to the board using a Series 220 Nylon No. 6 brush and Burnt Umber thinned with turpentine.

As this was a very small dog I decided to position it on the canvas in such a way that the viewer is looking slightly down on it, which helps to emphasize how small the dog is. Having carefully drawn the animal's outline and the shape of the eyes I put the dark areas in on his one black ear and its shadow beneath, the inside of the white ear, a bit under his nose, and on the lower lip and under his chin. Next the areas of background shadows behind and beneath the dog were rubbed in with a rag dipped in a thin solution of Black paint and turpentine.

As the dog was white I decided on a darker background to make him stand out. For **fig. 24** I first made a mix of white to which I added Viridian and Yellow Ochre. Using a Series 220 Nylon No. 8 brush moistened in equal parts of turpentine and linseed oil I started work in the upper left-hand corner of the canvas and gradually moved across the background of the picture using short, dabbing strokes. I added a little more Yellow Ochre where I painted down and around the tail. This colour mixture was taken down the right side of the picture and right round to the other side of the dog, but always leaving some canvas showing through to give an effect of lightness and sparkle. I did not fill in all the background at this stage of the painting, but turned back to the dog itself to paint in the darker tones of its fur. For these I added to the original mixture of Ivory Black and turpentine, a little Cobalt Blue and Viridian. With a clean No. 8 nylon brush I painted in the darker tones around the raised white ear and down the side of the head as well as the shadows beneath and between the front legs and under the body leading up to the hindquarters.

I then mixed Cobalt Blue with Cadmium Yellow and a little White and worked down the right side of the canvas and around the dog and along the base of the picture to fill in the rest of the background. If your colour seems too strong, add a little more White until you have the desired tone of green. Where the darker and lighter tones meet in the

Fig. 22

background I blended them together with short, dabbing strokes, so that there were no hard edges. I used two No. 6 nylon brushes, one for the darker tones and one for the lighter. You should blend the dark tones into the light very gradually to get the same effect as in my painting (fig. 26).

Going back to the dog, a smooth underpainting of white was applied on which the impression of rough fur can be built up layer by layer (fig. 26). With a Series 220 Nylon No. 6 brush, sparingly moistened with medium but well loaded with White, I painted the left ear. I worked all over the white areas of the dog always applying the paint thickly. I then painted the highlight on the edge of the flap of the black ear. Some of the initial guidelines of the original drawing could be overpainted here as there should be no hard edge showing around the dog in this final stage. The

dark tones which occur just above the root of the tail and extend along the right side of the hindquarters, haunch, stomach and under the chin were filled in by adding a little Burnt Umber and Black to the white mixture. These darker tones also need to be where the upper part of the front leg joins the chest and at the joint of the front paws and upper legs.

I then painted the dark ear in detail. Notice that it is made up of tones of black and grey, with the white highlight on the flap blended into the black of the outer ear. The tone inside the ear is an even darker grey. A touch of Crimson Alizarin with Burnt Umber and White mixed to make a pink flesh tone was applied just under the ear flap. A touch of this skin colour was also painted at the corners of the eyes and above the black at the top of the nose just

41

Fig. 23

Fig. 24

Fig. 25

where the hair divides. There is also a glimpse of pink between the central toes on each front paw.

I painted the nose with a diluted mix of Black and the medium, while the highlight was a pale grey (see **fig. 25**). I purposely did not paint the highlight white as it would have looked too bright. The outline of the nose and nostrils was painted in Black with a Series 133 Sable No. 6 brush. As always the whole expression of the animal is dependent upon a good portrayal of the eyes. These had already been drawn in so it was just a matter of filling in the details. The whites of this little dog's eyes show very clearly against his brown pupils. These whites were painted with pure White with a Series 133 Sable No. 4 brush moistened with medium. The rich brown pupils were painted next, using a No. 4 sable brush and a mix of Cadmium Yellow, a small amount of Burnt Umber and a touch of Crimson Alizarin. The iris was painted in a curve with Black on a No. 4 sable brush, leaving the highlight clear. I added a touch of White into this highlight. Look closely at the detail of the dog's face to see how I painted his features (**fig. 25**).

Finally, I added the finishing touches to the dog's coat. Using a Series 220 Nylon No. 6 brush loaded with thick White paint (no medium was used to thin this down) I painted on layer after layer following the sweep of the hair growth. This should end up beautifully thick (*impasto*) so you feel that you can practically touch his rough, ragged coat!

Fig. 26

PORTRAYING EXPRESSION

In successfully capturing an animal's expression you are bringing a picture to life and so the expression is often the single most important part of your picture. This is true at each stage from the initial drawing to the final touches of colour or shading.

The Eyes

An animal's eyes tell us most about its character or mood and must be drawn very accurately. It can be useful to sketch the eyes and indeed the whole head separately on a larger scale to the rest of the picture in order to grasp the subtle lines which mean so much. Use a sharp pencil or pastel, a fine charcoal stick or a small sable brush to draw the lines clearly. Drawing the same animal in several different moods helps you to understand the slight variations of lines which produce different expressions.

First check the size and position of the eyes in relation to the other features of the head. How far apart are the eyes? Perhaps they are set at a slight angle or V-shape, to the nose. If so, how pronounced is the angle? Then look at the curve of the upper eyelid compared to the lower. If the upper lid is arched the animal may look quizzical, friendly or perhaps sleepy (see **fig. 27**).

In dogs this could be accompanied by drooping jowls beside the mouth and pouches or bags under the eyes, as with the Bassett hounds in **fig. 28**. If the arching is more pronounced the animal might appear to be staring intently at something. On the other hand, a straighter look to the upper lid may make the animal seem wary or even angry. This particularly applies when drawing cats. A concentration of shadow here would enhance the slightly frowning appearance. This is useful if you want to show a cat about to pounce on something which has riveted its attention – for example, a ball of wool. The eyes of a Siamese cat would be set close together and the pupils would appear to point inwards, making the cat look cross-eyed. Remember, too, that cats' pupils dilate in the dark and are just slits in bright light.

An important factor in portraying a dog's expression is the amount of shadow and detail around the eyebrow follicle, situated above each eye.

Also, the more circular a cat's or dog's eyes appear, the franker or more playful the animal looks. This is particularly true of kittens or puppies. Care and accuracy are needed, however, since it is unlikely that the eyes will look perfectly circular. The size of the pupils must also be checked as you don't want the animal to look as though it is staring.

Fig. 27

Not all expressions can be described in human terms such as trusting, affectionate or playful, but all can be depicted, in any animal, by carefully looking at the give-away signs in the shape of the eyes. Showing whether they are round, narrowed, arched or oval-shaped is the first step to capturing an expression.

You must also be accurate in drawing the corners and tear-ducts of each eye to complete the eye shape. Is the tear-duct level with the outer corner or lower than it, so making the eye seem angled or slanted? This simple feature could change the animal's whole expression. Check also that you have created a *pair* of eyes rather than two that don't match. They won't match if one is level and the other slanted, for example, or if one is nearer the nose than the other. However, they may not be perfect replicas of each other since your position in relation to the animal will make the drawing of each eye slightly different.

After the drawing, the next important stage comes in the colouring and shading of the eye and in showing its highlight. Be careful in positioning the highlight and in gauging its intensity as incorrect placing of this highlight will alter the whole expression. It may be altogether too harsh to place a highlight on the pupil in pure white. If you are using white paper you may wish to leave the

Fig. 28

highlight unpainted initially and later paint a pale, transparent wash over the whole eye or shade it very delicately. This would tone it in slightly, but still leave it sufficiently distinct and alive. Alternatively, it may be blended in with the colour of the iris at one side; this too will lessen its harshness. Whether an animal is in bright light or in the shade, whether it is alert or sleepy – all these factors will affect how strong you choose to make the highlight.

Again, remember that the eyes must be treated as a pair, so both highlights will almost certainly be placed and treated in a similar way.

In painting the rest of the eye the choices are the same. It is usually better to paint a few shades of similar colours blended together than to paint one colour which would make the eye look flat and lacking in depth. Here again a transparent overglaze might help. Look at the Alsatian in oils on pages 32–35 and note the way I painted his very expressive eyes.

The Head and Body

Naturally the eyes are of paramount importance in getting an animal's expression right. But there may be pointers in the mouth, nose, ears and elsewhere which would reinforce the expression you have depicted in the eyes. Perhaps you

can show a puppy's lopsided grin or the set of its ears. The alert ears of a Doberman would require different treatment from those of a terrier that had one ear erect and the other lying flat. A horse's ears can tell us a lot about how it feels. If they are lying back against its head, with eyes wide and nostrils flaring, it is either afraid or annoyed and should be comforted or left alone to calm down. However, when a horse's ears are pricked forward it means that the horse is alert and inquisitive (see the picture of the mare and foal on page 53).

Having tackled the drawing of the head, look again at the body to see if it mirrors the facial expression in any way. Concentration in the eyes may be supported by tenseness in the body: an action suspended or about to happen. A sleepy animal's whole body will be relaxed and may seem a soft bundle of curved lines and fur.

All of these points are simply a question of careful observation and accurate drawing. Checking relative positions, sizes and angles methodically will eventually produce an instinct in you for what is essential in an animal's expression. There is no point in tackling points of detail elsewhere until you have first attempted to capture the expression. But once you have caught this you can feel confident that you have brought your picture to life.

45

PORTRAYING EXPRESSION
MY PUPPY TESS
IN PASTEL

Fig. 29

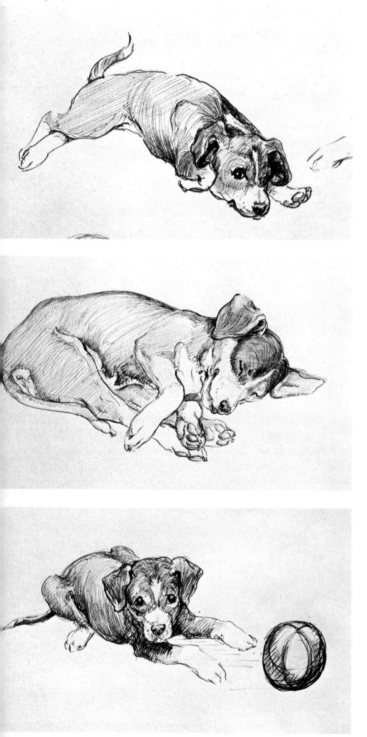

I've had Tess since she was just six weeks old. She was the ideal subject for painting because she was so adorable and I was determined to capture her personality and character in a picture. While playing she would suddenly flop down, her legs and paws at all angles. Using a large sketchbook, I did a number of sketches on each page as she changed position. I talked to keep her attention and she very soon realized that I wanted her to keep still. She learned quickly.

The three drawings on this page (**fig. 29**) were done with a medium-tip black ballpoint pen and coloured with pastel Yellow Ochre Tint 4. For the darker areas I used sanguine Conté, with Burnt Umber Tint 4 for the eyes and Madder Brown Tint 2 for the protruding tip of her tongue and her paw pads. I planned to make the final pastel painting one of Tess in three completely different poses. After I had done several drawings of her in different positions I grouped them together and rearranged them several times. I finally decided to use one of her lying on her tummy looking soulful; one of her asleep curled up with her paws in a heap and her tongue protruding, and one of her half sitting up. As you will see in the original drawing she had a ball in front of her to show how small she was in proportion to it.

However, despite much arranging and rearranging the drawings did not seem to group well together. So I made myself a mug of coffee and walked round the garden, trying to clear my mind and work out the problem.

Back at the easel I suddenly realized that it was the ball which made everything look wrong. This odd shape was out of keeping with the rest of the forms, so I removed it. However, this presented me with a new problem: Tess's far front paw seemed to lead the eye out and away from the picture. Then I remembered her habit of crossing one paw over the other. It took only a few moments to alter the position of the paw and suddenly it had all fallen into place. This exercise in composition illustrates the importance of preliminary sketching and careful observation. And as I've said before, if something doesn't seem quite right, go away from the painting, do something else and clear your mind, then when you return to the painting you can look at it with a fresh eye and, hopefully, spot the error.

Now for the final painting of Tess (**fig. 30**). I chose a sheet of medium-thickness Fabriano 160gm² paper, size 50 × 70cm (27½ × 19½in). Using a 4B pencil, I very lightly and carefully drew in the three poses I had decided on, making sure that the drawing and placing of each pose was correct by constantly referring back to my sketches. When building up such a picture, great care must be taken in forming the basic shapes and when using pastel and charcoal you must be very careful not to smudge your work with your hand. Using a finely sharpened black charcoal pencil I went lightly over the 4B pencil guidelines. Now I had to show the contours of the body, which were gradually worked in using the charcoal in fine lines to follow the growth of the hair and show the bone structure and muscle formation underneath. With white Conté I put in the light areas on the back of her head, paws, legs, and the small white feather shape on the back of her neck. The light golden brown markings were filled in with Yellow Ochre pastel Tint 4, and where these tones darkened into shadows, sanguine Conté. The nose in each case was carefully drawn with a sharpened charcoal pencil. In each pose there is a two-toned highlight showing across the top of the nose, and round the nostrils (see **fig. 31**). For the mid-tone I used Cool Grey pastel Tint 4 and for the very light tone, white Conté. I finely sharpened my black charcoal pencil and drew in the shape of the eyes; first the eyeball, and the upper and lower eyelids which slightly overlapped the eyeball above and below. Then I painted a narrow curve of Yellow Ochre pastel Tint 4 around the base to half way up either side of the eyeball.

When drawing the pupil I again used the sharpened black charcoal pencil filling in from the base towards the centre where I left a small area of the basic grey paper uncovered as the highlight. This in turn had a tiny dot of white Conté placed where more light was reflected. Finally, I put a touch of sanguine Conté at the inner corner of the eye, against the tear-duct.

I think a dog's paws are very appealing, and Tess's were particularly so when she was a puppy. Her toes needed careful observation, with special attention given to the drawing of the toe-nails, the way they fitted into their sockets and their delicate creamy-white colour. The pads were smoothly-shaped ovals and the central pad, equivalent to the palm of the human hand, softly curved. Each pad was separated by very short, velvety hair. I painted the pads with Madder Brown Tint 2 and added a touch of white Conté where the light caught them. For the darker areas around her muzzle I drew tiny overlapping lines with black charcoal pencil. The tongue was painted with Madder Brown Tint 2 and I darkened it just under and against the upper lip with a touch of black charcoal pencil.

I worked all three poses more or less together, going from one to the other so that the effect was gradually built up evenly over the whole picture at the same time. In this way you maintain a feeling of unison despite there being three separate poses. I gave the bodies weight and form by using the flat side of a broken black Conté in sweeping curves which followed the shapes of Tess's form. In the dark areas I gave extra depth of tone with Ivory Black pastel slightly pressed (not rubbed in) with the tip of a finger, and then worked over it with a fine line, here and there, of black charcoal pencil.

Fig. 30

Fig. 31

PORTRAYING MOVEMENT

The time will come when you decide you want to capture the likeness of a moving animal in a painting. It could be of a horse trotting, or a dog or cat running. Whatever animal you are trying to show in motion, you should think fairly carefully about how to portray it. A painting is after all flat and still (two-dimensional) so any attempt at capturing something solid and moving will involve some measure of illusion.

Firstly, you must understand how the animal moves. Different animals move in different ways. Their movement also changes according to how fast they are going: for example, a horse's walk involves a different sequence of leg positions to its trot and its gallop. When an animal walks some of its feet will be touching the ground but as it runs or gallops there will be moments when none of its feet are on the ground.

Observe as much of an animal's movement as you can before you start to draw. Then do several quick sketches with a fibre-tip pen, pencil or some other medium which enables you to work swiftly. Don't worry if the sketches are unfinished. You should be able to extract the most important parts from different sketches of similar movements and then combine them into one which should depict the desired movement accurately. Such quick sketches often have a flowing action to them which is part

Polo 41 × 51cm (16 × 20in)

of your instinctive and rapid response to a moving subject. These help create the 'feel' of the action. If you choose to supplement your study of animal movement by looking at photographs and drawings in books do not forget that your original, unfinished sketches from real life may well have captured the essence or illusion of movement and something of them will be needed in your final work. Essentially, a photograph is unselective whereas a drawing selects – even if the decisions and choices made are instinctive. A photograph shows every detail in sharp focus, it freezes the action; a drawing can show the important overall impression and you may choose to eliminate unimportant details which clutter the picture.

If you choose not to aim for the still, frozen image, you will have to decide which details can be suppressed. For instance, is it important to show the ground under the animal's feet? A foot touching the ground may anchor the picture and destroy the sense of movement. It is helpful to suggest the shape of a paw or hoof but it may be unnecessary to show every detail. On the other hand, details will still be needed on the face and head: the eyes will show the animal's personality, the ears may lay back along the head if the animal is moving very fast.

Generally, more detail will be shown in an animal that is walking than in one that is running as fast as it can. For a walking animal the 'frozen image' may be acceptable, and consequently presents fewer problems to the artist.

When portraying fast movement (see *Polo*, this page) hard contrasting colours should be softened and body colours blurred together or streaked slightly. If pencils, pen or pastels are used, shading may be done by lines drawn very close together rather than a solid shadow. In watercolour or oils you can consider leaving the sweep of the brushmarks subtly showing through but they must follow the direction of movement. If you feel technically competent enough, you may endeavour to create a very slight blur of movement, especially around the feet and away from the head. This would be in a softer, lighter version of the body colour with no sharply-defined lines.

The lines of the body should be seen to flow. They should form smooth curves and not be used to sharply define each individual muscle. They may fade slightly on the tail and ankles as they do in the ballpoint pen drawings of the greyhounds on page 49, but need to be strengthened where they are most important – on the spine. A line which is too broken will destroy the movement; but equally a continuous outline may deaden and flatten it. As always it is a question of balance.

A running or galloping animal is an animal of extremes. Its muscles bunch and tense ready to spring, then extend outwards in a leap. This process is repeated continuously. As a greyhound's body tenses the legs bend in under its belly, the spine is arched, the neck and head held up slightly. In the long stride that follows the body straightens, head and front legs extend forward almost touching each other, backlegs extend full stretch behind. At neither

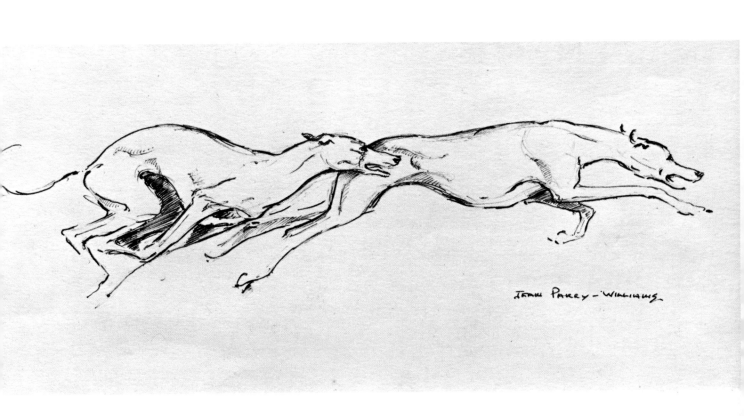

extreme do the feet touch the ground (see my pastel painting of greyhounds racing on page 51). Similar observations can be made for cats, horses, rabbits etc., although each will have its own particular strides, paces and muscle patterns.

At various points between the extremes mentioned the feet do touch down, often in sequence but not in unison. Curiously, it is preferable to draw the front feet touching down at the end of a leap rather than show the rear feet still on the ground at its start. This somehow roots the feet to the spot so that rather than creating an illusion of movement you create one of a sculptured animal on tiptoe reaching out but not moving.

Other things also help to create an illusion of movement. For example, a horse's mane and tail. The mane streams wildly out behind the head and the tail is raised to about 45 degrees when the horse is cantering or galloping. Also, if you are painting a picture of, say, a show-jumping scene, you will need to observe the way a horse's legs tuck under its body as it clears the jumps. Similarly, you will have the position of the rider to examine. Is he or she seated in the saddle, or, when jumping, propelled very slightly out of the saddle? The faster the horse goes, the more the rider leans forward against its neck. Reins will be held tightly and will not be slack. All these points should be carefully noted.

While all drawings of moving animals pose special problems, there are fewer if you are doing a profile. For reasons of dramatic impact or to record a particular observation, you may choose to draw a more complex, front-on view.

Moving animals seen head-on or at a slight angle present all the problems of foreshortening with little of the predictability that a stationary animal might have. For this reason I recommend you be very self-critical in your observations and take nothing for granted. Use photographs as an aid if you wish. The size/comparison method of drawing proportions (see pages 16–17) is a useful tool under these circumstances. Often a large expanse of body will be compressed by foreshortening into a small space in your picture. By comparing it with, say, the head size, you can eliminate any distortion that may make your picture seem ridiculous to someone who is more familiar with the animal than you are. This way of portraying movement is more difficult than doing a profile view and takes time, practice and confidence to perfect – but it will come in the end!

Finally, there is the question of background. Do you want to include one at all? If so, how detailed should it be? A clear, sharp-focus background presumes the time to observe it; in other words it is slightly alien to the idea of speed of movement where details are blurred. Consequently, such a background would only be used if the movement was slow because it would have an anchoring effect.

It is clear, then, that depicting movement requires careful observation and a knowledge of your subject. Equally it involves artistic judgements of selection and refinement. When these come together successfully into a finished picture the result is one of increased impact and drama and you can feel satisfied with a job well done.

PORTRAYING MOVEMENT
GREYHOUNDS
IN PASTEL

I will now describe to you how I painted in pastel the running greyhounds in my painting, *Running Free*. I first made a quick sketch with black ballpoint pen of a single, racing greyhound (below) showing the outlines of the

jacket and muzzle. Next I drew two hounds wearing racing colours and muzzles, each in a different position with one just ahead of the other (**fig. 32**). This created a feeling of continuity and forward movement which would have been lost if there was a space between the dogs. For this drawing I used black ballpoint pen and coloured pencils. For my final preliminary sketch I drew the two greyhounds in the same position as in the second sketch, but without their racing harnesses.

Then I had to choose a suitable paper. First of all I tried a fawn Ingres paper but this colour did not look right with the silvery grey tones of the hounds, so I decided to use a blue/grey Ingres paper. I planned to have a slightly darker grey mount with a silvered frame.

I pinned the blue/grey Ingres paper to my board and lightly drew in the outline of the animals with a 4B pencil. When I was satisfied that the drawing was correct I sharpened a medium black charcoal pencil and carefully drew over the pencil outline of the hounds again. Before you actually start to paint in pastel it is important to test the

Fig. 32

colour of your pastel on the edge of the paper you have chosen to see how it will look before applying it to your drawing. Pastel can look quite different on various shades of paper. For instance, the Purple Grey Tint o has a mauve tone when applied to white paper but on blue/grey Ingres paper it gives just the right impression of the silvery grey of the greyhound's coat. The testing of pastel colours is especially necessary if you are using a shade of paper different to the one that you normally use.

As you can see, both greyhounds have very pale coats (see **fig. 33**). For the rear greyhound I chose a Cool Grey Tint 2 pastel to fill in the main form. I broke the stick in half and using the side, swept in the shapes of the large muscles, along the neck, over the shoulders, the rib cage and along the flank. With the edge of my finger I then smoothed the edges of the applied pastel so that they softly blended into the paper without leaving a hard edge. This helped to give a feeling of solidity to the moving body. Next came the richer half-tones where the form curved in, and for these I used Vandyke Brown Tint 1 and again used

the edge of my finger to blend in the colours.

For the leading greyhound I changed to Purple Grey Tint o. I worked this over the body in the same way that I painted the other dog, again using the tip of my finger to work in the edges of the form. Where the tones became lighter I used the side of a broken piece of Silver White pastel. I varied the effect of light and shade on the charcoal pencil lines by decreasing and increasing the pressure of the stroke. The darkest shaded areas on both hounds were hatched in with the same charcoal pencil, i.e. fine lines drawn very close together. I painted the lightest highlights on both hounds with white Conté.

With the exception of the strengthened black drawing lines, and the dark hatched shadows, the whole picture was worked in very pale tones so that when it was finished, mounted and framed, the effect was a harmonious blend of pale colours.

The impact of the painting lies in the variations of weight in the light and dark charcoal lines, and the rhythm and sweep of the movement of the dogs.

Fig. 33 *Running Free* 41 × 76cm (16 × 30in)

PAINTING BACKGROUNDS

Your success in painting and drawing animals will undoubtedly be enhanced if you understand the importance of viewing your picture as a whole. For every painting you will need to decide whether or not a background is required. If you are sketching an animal, or a group of animals, a background will be needed only in so far as it adds to the information you are collecting in your sketch. Most paintings which are taken beyond the sketch stage will, however, need some form of background to make them complete, even if it is only a suggestion as in the watercolour sketch of horses grazing in a field shown here. This is not just a matter of providing information about the animal's habitat but is important for creating a decorative setting for the painting.

Whichever type of setting you choose, it is wise to echo the colours of the animal in the background around it. If this seems difficult – for example, if you have a brown dog set against a green carpet – it should still be possible to harmonize the two by adding a hint of the brown to the green mixture, but not enough to change it completely. There *may* even be a few hints of a greenish mixture added to the shadows in the dog's fur, but this should not be overdone. A dog painted in warm brown colours would look stark and unreal against a plain white setting; so a warmer-coloured background would improve the overall effect of the picture enormously. Remember that brighter colours are more difficult to harmonize. Most colours in nature are not as pure as the colours of paints and pastels so it is beneficial for you to mix and tone down your colours if you are aiming at realism and colour harmony in your painting.

Is the animal the most important feature of your painting? If so, it will be detailed and prominent against a suggestion of a background which itself contains very little detail. This is frequently the case if you wish to capture the likeness of a pet or favourite animal in a portrait. For examples see my puppy Tess on pages 46–47 and the little white dog on pages 40–43. If, on the other hand, you are depicting a farmyard scene in which the buildings and farm equipment are as essential to your painting as the animals, you should treat each feature equally and none should be given undue prominence.

Basically, there are three types of background to be considered: outdoor, interior and abstract.

Outdoor Backgrounds

Some typical examples of outdoor settings are: a sheepdog at work herding sheep (see my painting on page 65), horses grazing in a field (this page), a puppy playing for the first time in snow, or a cat lying asleep in its favourite sunny spot in the garden. The choices are infinite, but a certain amount of critical observation, assisted perhaps by photographs, will bring your outdoor scenes to life.

Start with the horizon or skyline. A low horizon showing

your chosen animal tall against a plain sky gives the picture impact and immediately elevates the animal to a position of importance. For example, the watercolour painting of the steeplechaser, *High Clouds*, on pages 54–55 has a low horizon as the horse is of paramount importance in this picture.

Consider also the effects of light and the weather. You should know what sort of day you are trying to depict. Sunshine will cause strong shadows to appear in a painting if it is a bright summer's day. Shadows are longer when cast by an early-morning or late-afternoon sun, while at midday they are very short. They are softer and less noticeable if the day is overcast when there may be a more even, overall light. Colours are affected by these conditions, too. Grass may seem greener on a bright summer's day, duller and greyer on an autumn afternoon. All such details are important when painting an outdoor scene and you should always make notes about these things in your sketchbook so that you can incorporate them into your painting later.

Distance, too, alters the way we see things. There is less contrast the nearer one gets to the horizon; small details become invisible and differences are neutralized. Hills on the horizon merge into the colour of the sky against which they sit. So, on a bright day they would be bluer than on a dull day when they might look grey. In a bright evening sunset they might take on the reds and purples of the sky to the extent that they lose their own colour identity. The opposite is true as you move closer – details stand out more and everything retains its original colour.

Interior Backgrounds

An interior view will be used to show an animal's home or natural environment. It may be horses in a stable, as in my painting here of the mare and foal in their loose-box, or a dog in your living-room on his favourite armchair (which is probably yours, too!). A mischievous Siamese kitten may be better shown playing with a ball of wool than just sitting still on the floor.

It is important when painting backgrounds to take into consideration the light source. Is there a source of light creating contrasts between light and dark? In a stable we may see a single beam of light acting as a spotlight and catching a horse's face in great detail, but softening the background into subtle shades of colour where other objects, such as riding tackle, are only guessed at. This would be achieved by restricting everything to a very close range of dark colours and tones, perhaps six or seven similar mixtures, derived mainly from Burnt Umber, Burnt Sienna and Black.

Abstract Backgrounds

On the other hand, you may wish to omit all subject matter from the background and just use the colours of the animal to enhance its portrait in an abstract fashion. You can dab or stipple similar colours to those used on the body (as in

the painting of the Alsatian in oils on pages 32–35) to achieve a more abstract background. This stops the background being flat and boring but does not detract from the main subject. It is a good idea to place lighter colours in the background against darker ones on the animal and vice versa. The lower part of the painting should always be slightly darker than the upper to give weight to the whole painting (see the watercolour painting of Dinky the cat, on page 39).

Background Details

Just how much detail you include in a background is, of course, up to you. You must decide whether you are going to draw every leaf on a tree or just depict the larger patterns of light and dark. The problem can often be resolved by a clear understanding of your main aims and intentions. If you are predominantly interested in the animal's portrait you should limit your background detail to a minimum. If, however, it is a scene or pattern which contains an animal as part of the whole picture, rather than as its major feature, you should draw and paint detail throughout the foreground and middle distance.

It is in your choice of background that you make decisions that affect the overall look of your painting. Elsewhere, observation and accuracy are your watchwords, but here pictorial awareness is also called for. With practice, however, it is not difficult to make these decisions because you subconsciously become aware of which type of background suits your needs best. In reading this you have probably already dismissed some of the choices as not for you. On the other hand, an alternative may have been put forward which will seem attractive and which could give your picture added zest.

PAINTING BACKGROUNDS
THE STEEPLECHASER
'HIGH CLOUDS'
IN WATERCOLOUR

Fig. 34

Fig. 35

For this example of a painting with an outdoor background which I will take you through, I chose a fairly heavy rough surface Saunders watercolour paper (285gm²). It is expensive but well worth it for the extra control you have when using washes of colour. This paper is heavy enough not to need damping and stretching and does not cockle even after generous applications of water. It can be pinned straight on to your board. You can work the wet into wet method or dryer brush techniques equally well on this paper. It also takes light pencil work effectively and gentle rubbing out does not damage it.

The colours I used in my palette were: Ivory Black, Viridian, Cobalt Blue, Yellow Ochre, Cadmium Yellow, Lemon Yellow, Burnt Umber and Crimson Alizarin. No White was needed as I let the paper show through. I used only a Series 40 Sable No. 8 brush. The tip of the brush I used for very fine work and the full brush for broad sweeps and for thicker areas of colour.

First, decide on the height of your horizon. The horse should dominate and a low horizon emphasizes this. You will notice that throughout this painting I have moved from one area to another rather than finishing one section completely before going on to the next. There are two reasons for this - one is to allow certain areas to dry out so that a colour will not run into the adjacent one and the other reason is that it helps to keep the colours throughout the picture in harmony so that you can see how one will look against another as you paint.

Indicate the horizon lightly with an HB pencil and then carefully draw the outline of the horse using as few lines as possible (see **fig. 34**). Remember, once a pencil line is washed over with colour it cannot be removed, so you do not want unnecessary ones to show. Next draw in the landscape behind the horse with your pencil. Having done the preliminary drawing stand back and look at it. Now is the time to lift off any unwanted pencil lines with a putty rubber. It will be too late once you have started painting over the outline.

For the sky make a pale mix of Cobalt Blue using plenty of water and wash it across the top of the picture from left to right taking it carefully around and under the horse and overlapping into the trees, so that, when they are painted in, tiny gaps of sky will show through the foliage (see **fig. 35**). While the sky is still damp, run a stronger mix of blue into the upper section of the picture leaving areas of the paler tone to give the impression of clouds. With this same mixture, add the blue to the distant hills which show low down by the right-hand group of trees. Now start to paint the horse. Make a pale mix of Cadmium Yellow and a little Burnt Umber and using plenty of water and the tip of the brush, paint the ears and then, with a fully-loaded brush, sweep the colour over the whole body except the white blaze on his forehead and his mane and tail.

One point to notice: the hooves are hidden in the grass. If you were to paint them in it would immediately make the grass look like a flat carpet rather than growing grass. Obviously, if the horse was standing in a stable yard or on the road you would paint the hooves but not in this case. Now paint the group of tall trees on the left. For this you will need a mixture of Viridian with a touch of Cobalt Blue

Fig. 36 The steeplechaser *High Clouds* 41 × 51cm (16 × 20in)

and a tiny dip of Black mixed generously together using plenty of water. With dabbing strokes start at the top of the trees and fill in the big group, not forgetting to leave bits of sky showing through in places. Run the wash across and down to the base of the tree group. Repeat this with the clump of trees on the right of the picture. Then, with a paler shade of the same mixture, wash in the distant hills gradually fading them out where they lead across the horizon to the right. With the same pale tone, paint right across the centre of the field leaving areas of white showing in places. Now, rinse the brush and using Lemon Yellow and a touch of Cadmium Yellow flow a pale wash over the highlighted trees in the middle distance, working across the picture and also in the foreground as shown in **fig. 35**. With a little more Cadmium Yellow, fill in the yellow area where a mass of buttercups catch the light under the distant trees. Now return to the horse (see **fig. 36**). With Burnt Umber and a little Black, paint in his mane and tail. Leave the original pale wash as highlights on the horse. Generously mix Yellow Ochre, a touch of Burnt Umber and Crimson Alizarin for darker mid-tones on his head, neck and body. Enrich with more Crimson Alizarin for the broad pattern of strong darks on the legs and under the belly. Then mix Burnt Umber, Crimson Alizarin and Black and, using the point of the brush, draw in the nostril, mouth and eye, leaving the highlight on the eye pupil clear. Finally, add more Black for the darkest tones on the mane and tail.

Enrich the mixture with an addition of Burnt Umber and a little more Crimson Alizarin and run in the broad patterns of darker tones on the head, neck, the top of the shoulders, along the back and over the top of the rib cage, and the hindquarters. Then turn to the legs, darkening the distant fore and hind legs where they are in shadow. Strengthen the tone under the belly and again, where there is deep shadow at the top of the shoulder, the base of the neck, on the chest, and behind the forelegs where the belly starts.

Now to the final painting of the landscape. Make a wash of pure Lemon Yellow and paint the lightest tones of the trees in the middle distance right across the picture. Run some of this colour into the foreground and into the distant patch of buttercups. Add a little Cadmium Yellow to your mix, and then take this wash again over the lighter trees and the hills in the middle distance. This will add warmth to the painting. Now make a mix of Viridian with a little Black added and boldly paint the deep shadows in the foliage of the left-hand group of trees. Also wash this colour along under the hedgerows. Use a paler tone of this to indicate the clumps of foliage and with the tip of your brush paint the tree trunks in the right-hand group of trees. For the grass you should try to give the effect of clumps and tussocks – grass is never even and all one colour. Make a rich mix of Cadmium Yellow with Cobalt Blue, use plenty of water and paint the grass with short, sharp, brush strokes. Work in this way over and across the field from left to right. Shorten your brush strokes even more as you paint the foreground. Don't be afraid to allow white to show through here and there in the grass. It will add sparkle and brilliance. To finish, add a little more Black to the mix to make a very dark tone and paint the shadow cast by the horse.

EXERCISE FIVE
SIAMESE CATS
IN PASTEL

Fig. 37

Ideally, cats must be in a relaxed mood if you are to paint them well, so it is better to draw them in their own home and then paint them back at your studio. For this picture I did a number of quick sketches of the cats in different poses before making accurate drawings. As I was to paint the cats together, I had to decide upon the best composition. My final choice of positioning was to show two different poses with one animal almost in profile and the other in a three-quarter view (**fig. 37**). This is another exercise I will take you through step-by-step.

I chose a tinted paper (sand-coloured, medium-grained Fabriano Ingres as it provided a ready-made background on which the animals really stood out. These cats have lovely creamy colouring with dark points on their ears, masks, legs and tails. Their beautiful blue-green eyes show in fine contrast to the sand-coloured background.

Firstly, pad your drawing board with several thicknesses of newspaper, or any old scrap paper, so that if there are any uneven places on the board they will not make a bump in the Ingres paper. Also, it makes a more pleasant surface on which to work. Next, pin the Ingres paper over this on to the board with drawing pins, smoothing it as tight as possible with your hand. Do remember to wash your hands

before touching the paper as any grease from them will mark it.

I find it a great help to use an old mount, preferably in dark cardboard the size of the proposed picture, to frame the area on your paper where the cats are to be drawn (see page 17). In this case the mount would have to measure 25 × 41cm (10 × 16in). Place this 'frame' on your paper so that your eye will adjust to this size when drawing the initial outline. There is nothing more infuriating than sketching out your drawing and then finding it is too large or too small for the selected picture size.

Take a 4B pencil and lightly draw the outline of the cats, using very little pressure or you will dent the paper. When you feel your drawing is correct, lift off any surplus lines with a putty rubber to keep it as simple and clear as possible (**fig. 38**). It is much easier to erase errors at this stage!

With a penknife rather than a pencil sharpener (which will usually break the point) sharpen a medium black charcoal pencil and very carefully draw over the outline of the cats (**fig. 39**). Then shade in, with faint lines close together, the patterns made by the dark markings on the cats. Now fill in these lightly shaded areas with pastel

56

Fig. 38

Fig. 39

Burnt Umber Tint 4. You should then darken the ears, masks, legs and tails even more by working black charcoal pencil into the Burnt Umber Tint 4. For the cream body colouring on both animals use the side of a broken stick of pastel Yellow Ochre Tint 0. I often break a pastel in half and use the side rather than the tip for wide areas of colour as it gives a broader sweep of colour, ideal for emphasizing the contours of the body.

Now look at the eyes of both cats. They are made up of several colours. Paint tiny strokes of Coeruleum Tint 0, then Prussian Blue Tint 3 and, finally, tiny dots of Sap Green Tint 1 to add sparkle. The pupils are half-dilated and shown as a V-shape which you should draw in black charcoal pencil. The centre top of the V makes the highlight (see **fig. 39**).

You should now start to consolidate the work that you have already done. In this stage, (**fig. 40**), you want to give weight to the bodies, delineate the bone structure of both animals and their muscles and finally add the texture of the overlying fur. The dark markings on the heads outline the underlying shape of the skull where the smooth fur is stretched over the cheek-bones, nose and bones around the eyes. The different weight and strength with which you apply pastel can give the impression of different textures.

With Yellow Ochre Tint 0 and using short strokes to indicate fur, work over the light area of the reclining cat gradually building it up until it looks solid. Add a highlight on the shoulder, upper arm, forehead and stomach with White pastel. Then, with Burnt Umber Tint 4, blend along the back and into the cream of the body. You also need to consolidate the pale brown markings on the legs, tail, head and ears. For the mid-dark tones use Burnt Umber Tint 6 and for the deepest colour work in Black pastel. To give the effect of longer hairs over shorter, draw them in with tiny strokes of contrasting dark and light colours. The paw pads are drawn with black charcoal pencil and the highlights on the soft pads with Cool Grey Tint 4. Work the pink inside the cat's ears with Autumn Brown Tint 3 and tone into the dark interior with strokes of black charcoal pencil. Leave the final touches to the eyes until the next stage.

Now turn to the sitting cat. It is richer and darker in colour throughout than the reclining cat. To mould the face use strokes of black charcoal pencil enriched by the addition of Burnt Sienna Tint 8 on the forehead, muzzle and above the eye. This colour is also added to the black on the far ear. The front of the legs, paws and the hind legs are worked in black charcoal pencil, as is the tail and the line of the back. Now work Burnt Sienna Tint 8 into the back with strokes following the direction of the fur. Do the tail in the same way working along its length from root to tip. Then place highlights of Purple Grey Tint 2 on the legs, the paws and tail, and similarly on the forehead, nose and cheek-bones. Work the shape of the body with light, flowing strokes of Yellow Ochre Tint 0. Next, with Burnt Umber Tint 4, indicate the direction of the fur over the body and chest, particularly emphasizing the way the hair changes direction over the hindquarters, rib cage and stomach. Strengthen the colour where the fur folds in under the stomach with a few flowing lines of Burnt Sienna Tint 8, and draw some individual groups of hair on the chest and between the front legs using the black charcoal pencil.

For the pink inside of the ears use Autumn Brown Tint 3, and black charcoal pencil for the darker interior, indicating the moulding of the ear and the short hairs inside with the same pencil and a touch of Cool Grey Tint 2.

If you look at my final painting (**fig. 41**) you may think that there is not much difference between it and **fig. 40**. But if you look again there are certain changes. I decided that the nose of the sitting cat was too long, so I shortened the end of it and filled in more dark on the bridge of the nose. I also slightly exaggerated the moulding of the muzzle and made the upper lip more rounded, thus softening the cat's facial expression. The whiskers were also added at this stage; just touched in with very faint lines of a sharpened black charcoal pencil – you don't want them to look like steel wire!

I also decided to add some more detail to the reclining cat and, using the black charcoal pencil, I faintly drew in some long hairs where the hind leg joins the stomach, and indicated where the fur parts slightly between the neck and the shoulder. I felt that the sitting cat's body should look more solid and dark so I strengthened the dark areas.

The eyes of both cats needed a bit more colour so I added a firmer touch of Sap Green Tint 1, with the deep blue on the inner and outer corners strengthened with more Prussian Blue Tint 3. The upper section of the V-shaped pupils should be left clear, with the paper showing through as a highlight. The eyes of Siamese cats are beautiful and so I wanted to make sure that they really sparkled in my painting.

There are many little details and finishing touches to add to a painting that may seem finished at first glance. But don't be tempted to overdo the detail; it is sometimes better to leave a painting simple rather than add too many fussy touches to it. However, with practice you will know when to add details and when to stop. It's all a matter of observation.

Fig. 40

Fig. 41

EXERCISE SIX
MY DOG
IN OILS

Fig. 42

Fig. 43

One of the first reactions of the owner of a loved animal is to wish to have its likeness to keep for always. It is good to have photographs but to be able to make a drawing or painting is much more satisfactory. But how do we go about it?

It is really essential to make careful drawings of the animal in different positions because for a good portrait the pose must look as natural as possible. Look carefully at the different drawings of Dodie, my tricoloured Beagle (**figs. 42, 43, 44** and **46**). I wanted to paint her in oils but couldn't make up my mind on the best pose. Eventually however, I decided to use the pose where she is sitting up watching my every movement (**figs. 44** and **47**).

For my drawings, I used a large sketchbook, 4B and 6B pencils and a black ballpoint pen. I also used coloured Conté to lend a little touch of colour and give the drawings

a feeling of solidity and tone. It is useful to take down lots of notes about eyes, nose, muzzle, position of ears, details of legs and paws etc. as these will prove invaluable when you attempt the full portrait.

For my painting, I used a canvas board, size 51 × 41cm (20 × 16in), positioned on my easel lengthwise to best suit the dimensions of the pose. I left the canvas board white to lend brilliance to the painting and using a Series 220 Nylon No. 2 filbert-shaped brush and turpentine only for medium, I sketched in the pose. Be careful to position the animal correctly on the canvas allowing room at the top and bottom so the painting doesn't look cramped.

It is a good idea to start with a few guidelines to help you get the size and proportions right. For instance, Dodie's head is a blunt-ended triangle with the ears angled on either side. I dropped a line down the centre of the

Fig. 44

forehead to the nose and another from the middle of each ear to help me position the shoulders and forelegs. This line from the forehead also dropped down the nose and continued through the centre of Dodie's chest and acted as a guide to the placing of the hind leg and paw. The barrel shape of her tummy swung to the right with the powerful, muscled foreleg cutting across it. Her front paws turned slightly outwards. The foreshortened (see pages 18–19) right hind leg was angled in towards the viewer with the paw in three-quarter view coming in behind the right forepaw. The curve of her back swung down along the barrel shape and through the haunch and foreshortened hind leg and finished in the sweep of the tail.

It is important to note the comparative sizes of parts of an animal's body and the finer individual details that give the animal its character. For example, Dodie is fairly broad between the eyes: in fact almost the width of one of her pricked ears. There are slight wrinkles on her forehead and darker markings which extend down to her shiny black nose. The nose, viewed from the front, is heart-shaped and extra care is needed to portray this correctly. Her upper lip under the nose is gently curved and her muzzle very soft but well defined with prominent whisker follicles (see details in **fig. 45**).

Exactness in the initial drawing is all important because if the proportions are not correct at this stage the whole painting will be wrong, endless corrections will be necessary and as a result the spontaneity of the picture will be lost.

Step back and compare your work with your subject at every opportunity to check that you are progressing well.

The limited palette of colours I used throughout this

Fig. 45

Fig. 47

form – building slowly by degrees and not finishing one part before another.

Never work for too long at one time and take frequent breaks. When you return to your painting with a fresh eye you may be able to see alterations which are needed.

After I had filled in the main drawing and dark tones I started to work on the details. Dodie's white areas were painted with Titanium White, toned down with a touch of Yellow Ochre for the creamier parts and a little Black added for grey shadows. For the brown areas I used Yellow Ochre, with Cadmium Yellow added for the richer colour, and a touch of Crimson Alizarin for the deepest browns. The highlights on the forehead, ears, face and nose were pale grey, made by mixing White and a little Black. Dodie's darkest markings on her back and tail were done with Burnt Umber and Black.

The subtle details that make your animal an individual should be carefully noted. For instance, Dodie has certain characteristics which make her different – the way she sits, how she holds her head and ears and particularly her expressive eyes. The hair follicles above the eyes, corresponding to human eyebrows, hold particular expression in a dog, as does the set of its ears. Dodie's ears are soft and silky and her coat is thick with a sheen. These details need to be shown. Be careful always to follow the direction of hair growth with your brush strokes and note where the light falls so that you can pick out the highlights and tones of a coat. See pages 38–39 for more details on painting hair and fur.

I used cool grey (a mixture of White with a touch of Black) to highlight the pupil of the eye as this avoids the harshness of using plain White which can often give an animal a staring expression (see **fig. 45** for detail). Then I carefully painted the details of the black nose with grey highlights, grey muzzle, creamy paws and cream and black toe-nails to finish off the painting.

Finally, I studied my painting and checked every detail. All I needed to complete the painting was a suitable frame to complement Dodie's portrait.

painting were: Titanium White, Ivory Black, Cadmium Yellow, Yellow Ochre, Burnt Umber and Crimson Alizarin.

Having drawn the dog's outline on the board I took a Series 120 Nylon No. 4 brush and using Burnt Umber and turpentine as a medium I blocked in the main masses and shapes. I then started to put in the darkest darks and masses, using Series 220 Nylon flat, square-ended Nos. 5 and 8 brushes. I used a combination of Dodie's coat colours to paint a background of broken colour – Yellow Ochre, Cadmium Yellow, Burnt Umber mixed with a little White and Black – putting on the colour with short brush strokes. I was careful to place the dark background areas behind the lighter parts of Dodie and vice versa, thus managing to avoid a hard line but still making her stand out (see fig. 47).

After this initial work I went on to use equal parts of turpentine and linseed oil as medium and progressed with the picture working it all up together – background against

Fig. 46

EXERCISE SEVEN
SHEEPDOG AND SHEEP
IN PASTEL

Fig. 48

Fig. 49

I have often watched sheepdog trials and been fascinated and enthralled to see those patient sheepdogs rounding up and driving reluctant sheep into a small pen. It is a true battle of wills between the dog and the sheep. In this pastel painting I have tried to capture some of the atmosphere of the sheep stamping in anger, the dog creeping closer and

closer until, at the last moment, the sheep turn and bolt into the pen. For sketching scenes like this, either from the television or in the countryside, I generally use a black ballpoint pen and a Rowney spiral-bound sketchbook (PBS1). The pen flows easily over the smooth paper and it is an ideal medium for rapid sketching. I made a number

Fig. 50

of sketch notes of the sheep in many different positions and then made a rough composition of the picture to make sure that I had got everything in proportion.

On to a fawn-tinted Ingres pastel paper and using a 4B pencil, I copied very lightly the composition I had decided on from my sketchbook. I worked on the smooth side of the paper so that the lines would be easier to control (**fig. 48**). Any corrections should be made at this stage with a putty rubber.

With a sharpened medium black charcoal pencil, I carefully drew over the 4B pencil lines of the original drawing and lightly hatched in the dark areas on the animals. Then using a white Conté I filled in all the pale areas on the animals. I put no detail in at this stage (**fig. 49**).

It is at the final stage (**fig. 50**) that the picture is pulled together and strengthened. The sheep in the pen in the background are not painted in detail as the focal point in my painting is made by the sheepdog and the recalcitrant sheep in the foreground. The sheep-pen was given more definition by adding Burnt Umber Tint 4 on the shaded areas of the bars and then darkening them with black charcoal pencil. Next, I added a little more detail to the drawing of the group of sheep using the black charcoal pencil and working on their heads, ears, eyes and legs. For the bulky bodies covered with fleece I used Vandyke Brown Tint 2 and for the darker mid-tones, Madder Brown Tint 0. I used Yellow Ochre Tint 0 for the highlights.

I then turned my concentration to the single sheep in the foreground and drew it in detail with the black charcoal pencil. First I worked the ears and head, taking care to show the skull formation beneath the smooth dark hair on

the head. Note the U-shape of the nose and beneath it the central line above the upper lips where they curve away on either side. Notice also the way that the ears lie at an angle of almost 45 degrees to the head. A horse's ears, for example, are more upright in comparison. I emphasized the curls of fleece with black charcoal pencil for the darkest areas, Vandyke Brown Tint 2 for the rich tones, Yellow Ochre Tint 0 for the creamy colouring, and Madder Brown Tint 0 and White (Cream shade) for the highlights. Other anatomical features to note are that sheep seem to have very thin legs compared to the weight of their fleecy bodies, but when they are shorn they seem more in proportion. They also tend to be knock-kneed but make up for this by having very neat little hooves! It is useful to make these kinds of observations in your sketchbook before you start drawing or painting, especially if it is an animal you have not painted before.

I drew the dog in detail with the black charcoal pencil. I filled in the dark areas of his coat with the side of a black Conté but left the paper showing through in places for the lighter tones. The sheen on the coat was laid in with Cool Grey Tint 4 pastel and the white markings were painted in with white Conté with a touch of Yellow Ochre Tint 0 pastel for added lightness in places. The dog's long curly fur and his heavy ruff around the neck were carefully drawn with a black charcoal pencil while his brown eye was filled in with Burnt Umber Tint 4 and the highlight with a touch of white Conté. I wanted to leave the grass impressionistic so this was just very lightly shaded in with pale Sap Green Tint 5 and the darker tones with Sap Green Tint 8 and black charcoal pencil. And there you have the finished painting – full of life and movement.

ACKNOWLEDGEMENTS

My special thanks for their unfailing help and patience in the making of this book are due to: Royston Davies; Joan Clibbon, Robin Wood and Cathy Gosling at Collins; David Rose, Peter Garrard, and John Youé and his team. Also, thanks to Michael Petts for the main body of the photographs, Tony Latham for the photograph on page 53 and for Figs. 16, 20, 21, 23 & 24 and Chromogene for the photograph of the polo ponies on page 48.

My sincere thanks also go to the following owners who kindly gave permission for the reproduction of the portraits and drawings of their animals: Mr & Mrs Austen, Mr & Mrs Blackman, Dr Evelyn Churches, Mrs Burton and Mrs Scouler, Mrs Clifford-Turner, the Goulbourne family, Miss Jennifer Hardy, Mr & Mrs Hope, Mr & Mrs Wallace Maddocks, Mr & Mrs Vickers, Mr & Mrs Chapman and Mr & Mrs Christopherson. Thanks also to *Leisure Painter* magazine for permission to reproduce the pictures on pages 16–19 and 60–63.

And I am particularly grateful to my family and friends, both two- and four-legged, whose encouragement and co-operation made this book possible.

WILDLIFE

Martin Knowelden

PORTRAIT OF AN ARTIST
MARTIN KNOWELDEN

Martin Knowelden was born in 1943 in Borehamwood, Hertfordshire, which was at that time still a rural community.

He cannot remember a time when he was not interested in drawing and painting wildlife – his mother still has a drawing of a mouse that he did when he was two. Animals featured in everything he did at primary school, even in a poster to advertise the school sports day that was set as a class project. As a junior schoolboy, Martin kept a menagerie of small creatures – newts, slow-worms, grass snakes, frogs, sticklebacks and mice – all caught locally. With school friends, some of whom came from neighbouring farms, he also learnt to hunt, often with ferrets, and to rear small birds of prey.

The young Knowelden's reputation as a 'mender of sick and lame birds' led to a succession of unusual house guests, the most notable being a jackdaw called Duncan which was hand-reared and lived free in the garden when not perching on Martin's head as he cycled to and from school.

It was at Borehamwood Grammar School that Martin was first introduced to pottery, carving, sculpture, the history of art and, in particular, the philosophy of Gustave Courbet. Later, in 1960, he was accepted at the Art School attached to Watford Technical College where he attained his National Diploma in Design (NDD).

After his first job with a local advertising agency he joined the TV Graphics department of the BBC. Two years later he returned to Borehamwood with a job at ATV (now Central Television) where he specialized in animation and programme graphics.

During these years Martin felt that both Borehamwood and he had lost touch with their rural beginnings, and in 1971 he formed a design and illustration partnership with designer Rupert Brown, setting up a studio on the banks of the River Stour in Suffolk. They undertook a wide range of work and the discipline of having to draw a hydraulic piston with an airbrush one day, followed by a cutaway of a medieval church the next, is something Martin considers the most useful experience for any·artist.

His involvement with wildlife publications stemmed from his first one-man show of paintings and drawings. A publisher asked him to illustrate a book on rats, and this led to a wide variety of book illustration.

Martin draws a clear distinction between illustrating (for books, magazines and advertising) and painting. He has had exhibitions of paintings, drawings and bronzes in Europe and North America as well as in the UK, most recently at the Tryon gallery, London. He is currently working his way through a series of commissioned works in oil, with subjects including salmon fishing on the Wye, Jack Russell terriers hunting, and golden eagles in Wester Ross. These commissions are sandwiched between a series of paintings for six children's books and a book on hunting birds.

Martin now lives in the village of West Wratting, Cambridgeshire, with his wife and their two children. He grows all his own vegetables and greatly enjoys cooking and winemaking. He loves poetry and jazz and follows a wide variety of country sports. He breeds lurchers, keeps ferrets, and is an experienced falconer.

With scrupulous attention to detail Martin Knowelden offers in his wildlife paintings a very personal view which combines quite opposing elements. His treatment of animals in their natural habitat is sometimes hard and always unromantic, often revealing the harshness of life in the wild. The beauty of nature is always clearly present, however, and his work shows a sincere respect born out of his knowledge of this world. He quite obviously delights in the minutiae of his subjects, sometimes taking an almost microscopic view and delineating every pore and whisker. He has an unfailing eye for the unusual pose or situation, the incongruous prop and the intriguing composition, and includes in his paintings a wealth of subtle details, some of them decidedly tongue-in-cheek, to intrigue and puzzle the viewer. His work not only shows quite clearly his love, and his knowledge, of his subject, but also his love of paint. The play of light and shade, and the visual effects created by water are two recurring themes among many which demonstrate his genuine delight in capturing his quarry as a highly original image on paper or canvas.

Fig. 1 Martin Knowelden at work in his studio

SELF-PORTRAIT

I cannot recall a time in my life when I was not drawing animals and birds. Growing up in a little Hertfordshire village which was beginning to expand with London's overspill, I, and my friends, resorted to the countryside at every opportunity for our recreation. We knew where to go to watch badgers and the ways of foxes. We tracked roebuck and rabbits and kept mice and slow-worms in our bedrooms. I helped the injured and sick wildlife of all kinds and made ready use of the opportunity it afforded for close and careful study. I thought the first kestrel I reared and trained the most exquisite thing in creation and I have re-expressed that feeling with all the wild creatures I have ever come close to.

Much of the time that I was not actively abroad in the countryside, I was at home with pencils and paints, trying to draw it, and the animals that lived in it. I was continually frustrated by an inability to achieve on paper the beauty and vitality of the creatures I saw in the wild and, eventually, I found myself studying the wildlife about me with the express purpose of drawing and painting it more perfectly. The number of the halt and the lame (mostly birds) I collected increased and a rather gruesome collection of bones, teeth, wings and claws began, to which I am still adding today. Although I did not appreciate it at the time, and simply studied and drew nature because it was an enjoyable preoccupation, I realize now the distinct correlation between observation and the quality of my drawings. It is true for all artists, whether professional or amateur, that the best of their work will be that which is most carefully and sympathetically observed.

I am still frustrated by the gulf between my paintings and the reality, but we learn from each picture done and, hopefully, improve as we learn. While I know that perfection is unobtainable, striving for it remains exciting and inspiring.

Not only does the desire to paint animals demand study and research, but the techniques of using paints and brushes, pencils and paper, watercolour and washes need practising and perfecting. There are so many permutations and possibilities to explore, and each one of us must find the most successful, the most suitable for himself. Developing a style and applying it to a particular subject like wildlife can be the most satisfying of achievements.

I must leave research and study for each of you to work out for yourself. Circumstances, opportunity and commitment will decide for you the amount you need to do, but the techniques and the tools, the order in which things are best done, and the rules and guidelines within which your work will be achieved are much the same for all of us, and I can describe those which I have found most useful in the hope that they form a base on which anyone can build a style of their own. Let us now consider a general approach to wildlife painting.

I have always delighted in the machinery of painting. The textures of watercolour paper, the shapes of palette knives and scrapers, the brilliance of a new canvas – the list goes on. Equipment becomes worn and polished with time and patinated by paint and spirit, and familiar tools fit the hand comfortably, becoming irreplaceable allies in the business of making pictures. Get to know your equipment in this way. Enjoy using your tools and practise until you no longer need to think about them but can work automatically, the brush or pencil becoming an extension of your hand. You can then give your whole

attention to the painting itself. The worth of a wildlife picture is in the quality the artist imparts to his subject which makes it not merely a representation of a creature in the wild, as is a photograph, but suggests the character and nature of that creature, and makes the viewer aware of the intangibles. A good picture shows, within its forms and composition, the grace, the power, the intelligence: abstracts which can never be delineated, yet are clearly there in the 'mood' of the piece. It should contain the essence of its subject, make a definitive statement. With these problems to ponder, as you work at your canvas, you do not want to have to worry about which way up the brush goes!

What I have tried to do in this book is describe, from my own experience, the practices involved in gathering together all the separate threads that finally make up the finished work. Starting with field notes and sketching, through studio drawings and studies, and finally composing and executing your picture, the procedures described here are all those I use myself and which resulted in all the pictures in this book.

Some techniques will come easily and others will most certainly not. Do not spend a lot of time, all at once, on those which prove difficult but, rather, work on them a little each time you sit down to paint. Remember that art is only 1 per cent inspiration and 99 per cent perspiration, so work – observation and practice – is the major requirement. Your skills will never develop without it. The more precision and careful study that you get into your preparations for a painting, the more depth you will impart to it. Finally, and above all, never let anything you do become a chore. There is no value whatsoever in a picture or a drawing that is finished reluctantly. Let all your work be, as mine is, the product of enjoyment and pleasure, and an abiding fascination in your subject.

Fig. 2 Martin Knowelden with his ferruginous hawk

WHY PAINT WILDLIFE?

The first images ever made by man were of wild animals. Captured in exquisite economy, using pigments on the smooth walls of caves, are scenes depicting our earliest ancestors and dotted with creatures recognizable still as zebra, buffalo, giraffe and all kinds of antelope. Men with spears, bows and clubs, accompanied by curly-tailed dogs, weave in and out of these panoramic murals. Why these images were created we can never know with certainty, yet, even before man had formalized his gods, he was recording a relationship with the wild creatures of his environment in colour and line. Since these earliest records, man's attitudes to animals have been complex and contradictory. Some suggest that these early paintings were inspired by a mystical belief that the capture of an animal's image was analogous to the capture of the beast itself. The qualities of wild creatures – the cat, the hawk, the jackal, the ram, the scarab beetle and the serpent – were apportioned to the deities of ancient Egypt, and their depiction as man-bodied and animal-headed reflects the complex interaction of man and nature as perceived by the artists and sculptors of that long-dead civilization.

Many primitive societies carved and painted the symbols of their worship in animal forms, and this 'totemism' is evident in the wealth of animal representation seen all around us today. The beasts of the primitive totem makers have their modern-day counterparts in the lion at Britannia's side and the American eagle, both symbols of strength, reliability and courage we all recognize. Behind them is a vast array of creatures, each with its special qualities, symbolizing all aspects of our own lives and embodying ideals that we might all aspire to. The symbols of trade and industry featuring animals are legion and there are countless examples ranging from these to the tattooist's art, with every conceivable sphere in between.

The Victorians' sentimentality saw in animal behaviour lessons and moral pointers for us all to heed; Aesop had shown this with considerable humour, and much more vigour, centuries earlier. Yet Gustave Courbet, the French painter who became the father of modern art, derived from his hunter's knowledge of wildlife, combined with his careful study of animal life as an artist, a clearer understanding of his own place in the great scheme of creation.

Whatever the reasons for attempting the painting of wildlife (and I suppose there are as many reasons as there are people wishing to try it), let us begin with the simplest of motivations, the easiest to understand: admiration. For example, one sees a simple admiration for such creatures, so at one with their environment, in the cave paintings at Lascaux, and I look for no deeper or more obscure reason for their creation. Whilst they may be much more, they are certainly a celebration of superior strength and speed; skills in coping with hunger, drought and weather; abilities for providing shelter and food for their young; and, above all, freedom under the sky. Wild animals have always fascinated and intrigued us and, for some of us, this fascination has manifested itself in a desire to capture, as did our ancestors, some essence, some definitive quality stated in colour and line. The act of painting a mammal, bird or fish in a way which sums up some fundamental quality of character is, in itself, an expression of admiration, and if the image so made imparts that feeling to those who see it after, the work is properly one of art.

At its very best, animal art makes a profound statement about man's relationship to the rest of creation. At its most humble, the artist simply uses the many beautiful colours and the myriad remarkable forms that nature provides as the basis, the foundation, on which rests his own desire to create.

Whatever the motivation, taking a sketchbook and field glasses into the countryside and collecting material for use in the studio, as well as the general study of nature with the painted image in mind, is an absorbing and satisfying pastime. With sufficient practice to achieve a commercial standard and with an understanding of the demand from so many areas for animal and natural-history imagery, there is no reason why your hobby should not also be a source of income.

Backgrounds

The way we see wildlife, as a general rule, is in brief, sudden glimpses. Human eyes are so placed that we have a field of focused vision of about 17 degrees and we scan our surroundings either by moving the eyes themselves or by utilizing the articulation of the head. When we suddenly catch sight of a wild creature, we tend to fix on the animal (and on its eyes in particular if possible), and everything outside that 17-degree field is perceived as blurred vision, unfocused and indistinct. The animal becomes a vivid, sharply defined object on a vague, soft background, like a sparkling gemstone on a velvet tray.

Backgrounds, then, seem to be seen as impressions and, for the purposes of impact in your picture, they are, with some notable exceptions, best kept less than sharp. Aim for bold colour and strong lines that lead the eye to the focal point of the picture plane, without distracting it with unnecessary detail. An equal degree of finish over the whole painting gives the eye no 'high point' to fix on, no contrast or conflict to resolve, and consequently the picture lacks power.

I always start an oil painting by deciding on an overall general colour, usually dark green or dark brown, and laying it over the whole picture area, whether paper, canvas or board, with a wide flat brush, say a Dalon D.88 $\frac{1}{2}$ inch (or 1 inch for larger pictures). I let the natural texture that the brush imparts form the basis for the background. Grass and rock require quite different surface textures, yet I form both by the same technique – rubbing or scraping away the dark base colour to reveal the pale surface colour beneath. Experiment with this 'drawing in reverse' technique on scraps of paper or canvas; it can be very effective. I begin painting highlights into this base, developing and detailing the most the areas nearest the subject of the picture. I then mix a very dark colour (enough to last, for it will be needed for shading over the whole work), which is sympathetic with the base colour, perhaps the same dark green or brown I began with, and add it as shadow, rounding out and giving depth to the forms delineated earlier.

Backgrounds are as varied as subjects and need a varied approach. Some subjects might require no more than a colour wash or 'tint' to offset the focus, while another might well demand a complex tracery of leaves, flowers, branches and grass. There are no hard and fast rules and you must decide for yourself just how far, or in what direction, you must go according to the particular piece you wish to work on, or your particular style. There are one or two basic pointers, however, well worth bearing in mind. The background of a painting functions as the setting for a jewel; the gold surround supporting a diamond. It must enhance and underline the beauty of the centre of focus; it must frame and isolate; it should lend importance, making the viewer aware that the subject deserves special attention.

Once you have a clear mental picture of how you wish your finished piece to appear, you should establish just how 'finished', how detailed and polished, your subject will turn out. The background should then be worked backwards, as it were, from this point, never competing with the subject by equalling its 'finish', yet complementing and encouraging it, making the total of the work more than the sum of the parts. Remember that cold colours – blues, greens and tints based on the blue end of the spectrum – recede; they seem to go back into the canvas as you look at it. Warm colours project; reds and browns and the tints from the spectrum's yellow end seem to come towards you as you view the canvas. Use this optical effect for your own ends: a fox hidden in the grass would appear much more hidden in brown or yellow grass than in spring grass, lush and green. The colour of the fox, being a warm colour, projects out of the canvas and the colour of the grass can either throw it into sharp relief (if it is green and therefore recedes) or can complement and soften the subject (if it is yellow or brown and projects with the subject).

Shadow can be used to increase depth, anchor an object to a surface, or describe or reinforce the form of a subject by the line it takes as it falls across your scene. It can also be used to emphasize the texture of a background and is, of course, a simple way of justifying a dark or black background for anything pale or white which needs a clearly defined edge.

WHAT EQUIPMENT DO YOU NEED?

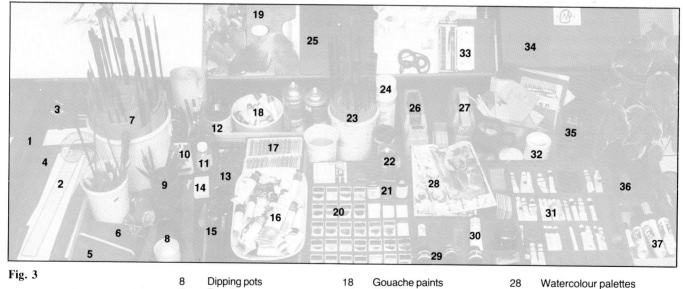

Fig. 3

Key to materials

1	Metre straightedge	8	Dipping pots	18	Gouache paints	28	Watercolour palettes
2	Perspex rule	9	Pencils	19	Oil palettes	29	Drawing inks
3	Mount cutter	10	Lighter fuel	20	Watercolour pans	30	Gel retarder
4	Cutting mat	11	Masking fluid	21	Varnishes	31	Watercolour tube paints
5	Desk brush	12	Linseed oil	22	Rotring inks	32	Paint wells
6	Emery cloth	13	Rotring compass	23	Watercolour brushes	33	Portable watercolour box
7	Brushes (Dalon) for oils	14	Putty rubber	24	Aerosol fixative	34	Portable oil painting set
		15	Palette knives	25	Sketchbook	35	35mm SLR camera
		16	Oil paints	26	Sellotape	36	Stapler
		17	Pastels	27	Draughting tape	37	Felt tip pens

Modern paints – oils, watercolour and gouache – are of superb quality, and while they may appear expensive as you survey the price list, a little goes a long way and they are, with proper use, very good value. A reputable supplier offers a huge range of pigments in several sizes and qualities, catering for amateur, student and professional artists.

Oils

Start with a comprehensive range of basic colours and wait until you have practised your palette for a while before you buy any of the more exotic colours. I would suggest you start with the primaries – blue, yellow and red – in two forms, 'hard' and 'soft'. I would describe Prussian Blue, Golden Yellow and Cadmium Scarlet as 'soft' primaries. Mixed with Zinc White (a 'transparent' white), they produce tints which are mellow and organic. Cerulean, Lemon Yellow and Rose Doré are 'hard' primaries. Derived, as most 'hard' colours are, from mineral or chemical pigments, they throw tints which are hard, clean and brilliant. These six colours should form the basic colour box to satisfy any requirement; simply add to these black and white.

It is as well here to describe the three whites. Flake White is a lead-based paint and, consequently, is dangerous if misused. It matures with a warm, amber tinge and is reasonably permanent, giving mellow tints and a 'glow' to work as it ages. It covers well used neat. (Permanence is the ability a colour has to remain as painted. Some violets and maroons change their colour very rapidly if left exposed to light; such colours are the opposite of permanent, i.e. fugitive.) Titanium White is derived from a mineral pigment and is brilliant and hard, giving off a lot of light. It, too, is permanent, although not to the same degree as Flake, and mixes a clean, sharp tint. Zinc White is produced with zinc oxide and is the least solid of the three. It is just as permanent as the others but imparts a translucent quality to its tints and can be used for building up layers of colour. Choose whichever white you feel most suitable (or buy one of each) and, with Lamp Black, your basic colour box is complete. I would, however, suggest that you add the earth colours – Vandyke Brown, Raw Sienna, and Yellow Ochre – and a good base green with very high permanence is Terre Verte.

You will also need a spirit in order to dilute your colour and an oil for your basic medium. Use turpentine for your diluent, and for your medium, linseed oil is unbeatable. For outdoor work or sketching, Gel Medium or Alkyd Medium mixed with oil paints are really excellent and dry in half the time oils take. Copal Varnish is a useful addition to your equipment, too. Thinned with turps, it can be used to varnish a finished work and, mixed with turps and linseed oil, it forms a beautifully smooth medium with

oil colour, allowing easier brushing and a faster rate of drying.

Watercolours and gouache

The difference between watercolour and gouache is in the nature of the paint itself. Watercolour gives a clean and transparent tint which is used as a thin wash on damped paper. The colour of the paper shows through and gives watercolour its luminous or glowing quality. Gouache is an opaque or solid pigment which is thinned with water and used on textured card or board, much as oil paint.

Brushes

Brushes, for me, are no longer the problem they were. The synthetic fibre used for many brushes is incredibly fine and ideal for oils; I use, now, nothing else. Even in the smallest sizes they are, in my opinion, the equal of any natural-hair brush and, what is more, they stand up even to my careless and heavy-handed treatment. (They come back to new with an occasional application of paint-stripper!) I have brushes from the whole range and I will pass on a useful tip here: get into the routine of buying one or two brushes each week and work your brushes in over a period. I try to avoid using a pot of brushes until they all need retiring and then having to start again with a brand-new set. It is also a painless way of renewing your most important item of equipment.

There is, of course, a great range of brushes and you must try several before you find the one ideally suited to your needs. I have found the perfect brush, for myself and look no further – you will find your own in time.

Watercolour, however, can only be worked with brushes made of natural hair, and very fine hair at that. Sable is incredibly strong and springy, considering the fine nature of the hair, and comes from a mink-like creature from Eastern Europe and China. Sable is extremely expensive and works quite beautifully, and a watercolour brush, carefully cleaned and shaped after use, will last for years. The less commonly used sizes and the big ones used for washes of flat colour are made in less expensive mixtures of hair without any loss of quality. I use pure sable, ox and sable mix, and some squirrel. Watercolours are notoriously difficult to control with inferior brushes, so make life easy on yourself and buy one or two top-quality sables.

Always clean your brushes thoroughly with a clean rag and whatever solvent is relevant: turpentine with oils, water with gouache or watercolour. While still damp, smooth and shape the brush, then stand it, bristles upward, to dry out naturally. A coil of corrugated cardboard held inside an old coffee tin makes an excellent brush stand, the handles of the brushes being pushed into the corrugations.

Pencils

Pencils, although the most commonplace of all an artist's tools, cause confusion and discontent. A pencil is a wooden sleeve surrounding a core of graphite mixed with clay. The wooden surround is cut away with a knife to expose the graphite core, which gives a black line. The more clay you mix with your graphite, the harder the core (or 'lead') and, consequently, the finer and paler the drawn line. The less clay in the mixture, the softer and blacker the line; simple, really. The hardness of a pencil is graded in degrees of H, the softness in degrees of B; an HB pencil is the average of the two. Buy hexagonal (easier on the hand) drawing pencils of the best quality only (buy cheaply, buy twice), in degrees HB, 2B and 6B. Shape your pencil point with a very sharp knife or one-sided razor blade to a long narrow point, the exposed lead being about a third of the overall sharpened tip. This allows you to use the sides of the pencil lead as well as the point. You will find a Black Beauty (an extra-fat 4B) very useful for filling in, and I prefer charcoal pencils to the traditional charcoal sticks. Kneaded erasers are useful for more than just erasing. They can be used as one would use white to draw into a sketch, or as a burnisher to smooth and soften pencil lines. All pencil, conté (a densely black wax crayon) or charcoal work needs fixing when finished to prevent smudging and you can choose a clear plastic varnish in an aerosol can or in a bottle with the old blow-pipe system.

Pens

Pens are a matter of personal preference. I do not like plastic pen holders as they are too short and too light (and plastic!), so I make bamboo holders of my own. I like the weight and feel of the wood and bamboo is non-tapering. I use sections of bamboo 10 mm ($\frac{3}{8}$ in) in diameter and 165 mm ($6\frac{1}{2}$ in) long. Gillott nibs are unbeatable and practice will indicate which grade suits you best.

Useful extras

You will find a number of odd tools very useful as you continue painting. A small, flexible palette knife, used to bring oil colours in from the edge of the palette to the centre for mixing, will keep colours clean and separate. A few scrapers for working into wet paint can either be made or found about the house. I have some sharpened bamboo, some old paintbrush handles with glued-in tips of bone and antler, and a variety of recycled knitting needles, chopsticks and screwdrivers.

Broken combs make lovely patterns drawn across the canvas, and old toothbrushes make good stipplers. All I can say about these gadgets is that you will know one when you see it.

A mahl-stick (the traditional artist's stick with a padded end) will keep your sleeves off your canvas when you work, will give you a straight edge for ruling brush lines or establishing horizontals and verticals, and will support your wrist for very small detail or precision work. To make one, use a metre (1 yd) length of 7 mm ($\frac{1}{4}$ in) copper tubing and bind on a chamois-leather pad at one end. Other useful aids are a pair of dividers, which will save you time and effort when transferring proportions on to the canvas, and, of course, compasses – very few people can draw a perfect circle freehand.

Save the plastic caps from aerosol cans; they make perfect dippers and you can discard any that become too encrusted. Rags are essential and must be free of any fluff which might transfer to your paint surface.

Painting surfaces

And now the problem of what to paint on. Water-colour papers are many and varied, giving more or less surface, greater or lesser strength, different degrees of absorption, and a wide range of textures. The prices vary considerably according to the structure of the material (paper is made from many different fibre types, rag being one of the best, wood pulp one of the coarsest) and the method of production (some are still hand-made). Once again the rule must be to try them and find out for yourself which is most suitable for your own purposes. An 18 × 24 inch pad is probably the easiest way to buy it.

For oils you have a choice of textures from rough to smooth, in canvas either ready-mounted on a stretcher or off the roll. Rough-textured is probably best left until you are well practised. Gesso is a very fine plaster and size mixture, resembling sour cream, which, used as a primer on your canvas, produces a surface as fine and smooth as paper. You can buy canvas, ready-primed, mounted on thick card squares, which are especially handy for outdoors or sketching. Gesso can also be used to prime hardboard or heavy cardboard, both popular and economical surfaces and both good for wildlife subjects because they are smooth and texture-free. There are many papers specially prepared for oil-paint sketching and you should buy a good block, say thirty sheets, 18 × 24 inch size, preferably with a waterproof jacket.

A drawing board is an excellent basic work-top and is easily carried with your paper in a sketching bag. It can be propped up on a table or used with an easel for painting indoors. Buy a wooden board, about 65 × 45 cm (25½ × 17¾ in). Easels come in a wide range of types and prices and you should choose the best you

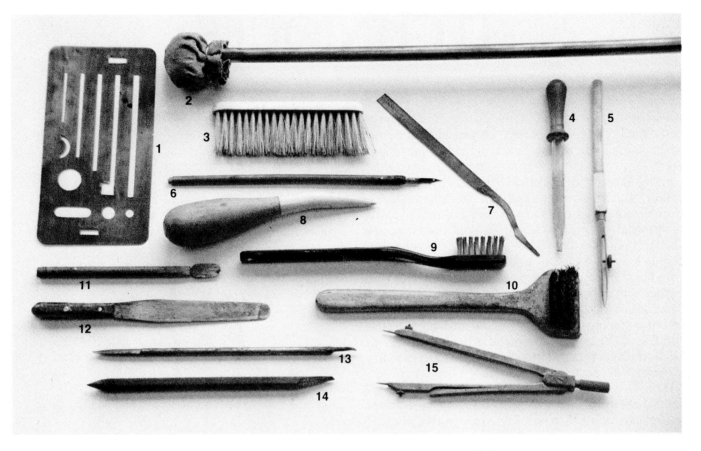

Fig. 4

1 Masking template
2 Mahl-stick
3 Small cleaning brush
4 Dropper
5 Ruling pen

6 Cane-handled mapping pen
7 Saw-toothed scraper
8 Burnisher
9 & 10 Brush stipplers
11 & 12 Mini palette knives

13 Brass scraper
14 Bamboo scraper
15 Dividers

can afford for the space you have available. If you want an outdoor one, a lightweight wooden sketching easel with collapsible legs and carrying handle is ideal. For indoors, something more solid is better.

All this is still only the basic equipment, and one of the great pleasures of painting is the accumulation of materials and tools. You will want, as time goes by, much which I have not mentioned here, and a good

relationship with your local art shop will prove invaluable. There are doubtless many items I would never think of using, which you will come to regard as irreplaceable in your paintbox.

Finally, take care when storing pictures. Watercolours should be kept out of the light, in a drawer, say, laid flat and protected by a sheet of tissue. Oils need to be stored upright and, when dry (sometimes this can take six months), varnished with a proprietary picture varnish of the brush-on or aerosol type.

TECHNIQUES

An artist's style – that which makes one person's work quite distinct from any other's – comes about because of the unique way in which each individual uses his or her tools. Van Gogh's short, stabbing, flat brush strokes, flowing in coils, or Seurat's tiny points of colour, mixing on the canvas, are both immediately recognizable. You must experiment and practise with the tools at your disposal and find out the range and versatility of each one; what each piece of equipment can do for you. I have a small watercolour box which I find invaluable for field notes and yet contains only eighteen quarter pans and one No. 4 round-end sable. These, I soon discovered, are sufficient for all the jobs I need doing out-of-doors, from colour washes to fine pen lines. A 5mm HB automatic pencil completes the kit, and I keep them all in a sketching satchel hanging, always ready, by the studio door.

You have only to look through an art supplier's catalogue to realize the vast range of tools and materials at your disposal. Experiment with as much as you can and try to reduce your requirements to a good, comprehensive, basic toolbox. Discover what serves your needs best and concentrate your practice on those techniques exclusively until they are second nature. When you are thoroughly conversant with your medium, like a musician who has mastered his scales, you can go on to improvise constructively.

The main tools of the artist are pencils and brushes, and the effects they can produce deserve some study. It is worth remembering that, artist or bricklayer, you should let the tools do the work for you.

Brush effects

In the case of brushes, practice will soon show you that one good-quality sable will give you a wide 'vocabulary'; a great range of textures and lines. Fill your brush with black watercolour wash and draw it across the paper from left to right at varying speeds. If it drips or splutters or in any way behaves on its own, take note how and why. It may well be of use. As the brush dries, gently splay out the fibres and see what marks you can achieve now. Lay the brush flat on the paper and roll it along. Discover the effects that you can get with the point, side, and flat of the brush, using it wet and dry alternately. Practise guiding your brush in as many different ways as you can and build up a set of practice sheets for reference. When you feel you have done enough with watercolour, begin again with oil paint, using turpentine substitute to thin your pigment to a wash.

Fig. 5   Fox and vixen: rendering the fur effect with a brush

Any new equipment requires practice to get the best results. Try another simple exercise: take a 12 × 18 inch sheet of watercolour paper and pencil in a grid, five spaces by five, giving you twenty-five squares. Take your new brush (or pen or pencil) and try to achieve a different texture in each square. A brush can be pushed as well as drawn across the page, and the tips of the bristles will give you stippling while the flat side gives you dabs of colour. Try your brush full of paint, then

Fig. 6   Flying duck: several different brush techniques combined to achieve texture and tonal value

again almost dry. Pin up this sheet of textures where you can refer to it when you come to your finished work.

Without practice you will struggle to achieve effects that with the right tools used in the right way you will find simple and quick; anything in your painting that is laborious or has been tedious to achieve will look like it. Wildlife, more than any other subject, needs to be spontaneous and full of life.

The watercolour sketch of the duck (**fig. 6**) illus-

trates the use of several effects coming from one brush. The textures of plumage, beak, leg and eye were all created using basically single-stroke work. The foxes (**fig. 5**), sketched after a farmer's shoot, were done with pen and ink, and I could well have spent hours rendering the fur had I tried to carry on with the pen. As it was, I used my brush again and rendered the fur effect in a few seconds. It also gives a far more convincing portrayal of the texture of fox-fur than any other method might have produced.

Fig. 7 Fine pencil

Fig. 8 Broad pencil

Pencil and pen effects

Fine pencil The beauty of a fine pencil is in its ability to achieve texture and tone by a series of criss-cross lines or 'hatching'. For wildlife studies, this technique gives marvellous precision for detail work. Keep a fine point on your pencil and a light touch, and build up density, as you would with watercolour, with a series of layers.

Broad pencil Strong, bold lines and areas of tone or shadow can be 'hacked' with a broad, soft pencil without wasting a lot of time. Use a long, tapering point and get your pencil to do the work by using the side of the lead as well as the point. Use your fingers to rub and shape areas of shadow. Aim to capture the essence of your subject in a few quick lines.

Fig. 9   Fine pen

Fig. 10   Broad pen

Fine pen   A fine pen is an unforgiving tool and de-mands practice to achieve worthwhile results. It is rarely used in my studio, but it gives an effect, like steel engraving, which is impossible to get any other way. The prime requirement for fine pen work is patience!

Broad pen   Any amount of finish is possible with a big nib, from loose, sketchy impressionism to highly finished realism. Use your pen freely and quickly, seeing what effects the pen itself can make. Develop and adapt those which suit your style best. Doodling is great practice.

81

ANATOMY

Just as you must practise a range of basic techniques to get the results you want from your equipment, so you must familiarize yourself with your subjects to achieve any worthwhile images. All creatures, in their construction, obey certain strict rules. Movement and form are limited by these underlying rules and the artist must learn what goes on under the skin of the creatures he wishes to paint if he is to impart any authority to his work, or bring any fuller understanding of his subject to the viewer.

Under the general heading 'anatomy', the artist should remember four elements which apply to fish, birds and mammals equally: frame, form, texture and colour. Let us look at each in turn.

Frame: the rigid skeleton which dictates the basic shape of the creature. Bones cannot stretch or bend so they give each animal a set of related measurements which are unchanging. Articulation is the movement of bones, one with another, at the joints. The remarkable complexity of bones in a bird's neck means it can articulate its head through 180 degrees and look directly backwards. The much poorer articulation of a toad's head means it must move its whole body to face in a given direction.

Form: the muscles which clothe the skeleton and give the animal a range of postures. There are certain poses characteristic of each specific animal, and the

Fig. 11 The underlying structure of a squirrel's frame (tail not shown)

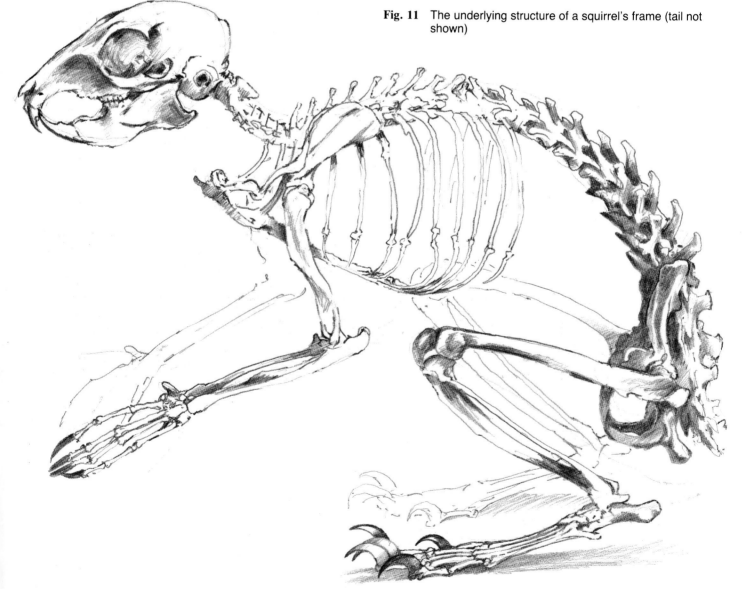

MAMMALS

changing shape of muscle describes activity or rest, anger or calm.

Texture: the 'feel' of the surface of your subject. Smooth fur, shaggy fur, smooth scales, rough prickles, wetness or dryness.

Colour: the artist must observe closely the colour of his subject. A white cat sitting in sunshine will carry gold and orange highlights and warm grey shading. In artificial light its colour will be hard white in illumination and a clean middle blue in shadow. Your subjects not only carry their intrinsic colour and pattern but take on the tints of reflected light from their surroundings.

The only way you will acquire the knowledge you need in the above categories is by studying, and a pencil and sketchbook should never be far away from you in case an opportunity for making notes or drawings comes along. If you have a dog or a cat, look carefully at how it is put together and how its tail, legs, ears, etc., join on to the trunk. Fish or fowl in the kitchen will give you a wealth of information as well as a good dinner!

Movement in an animal derives from its structure and should be most carefully portrayed. Until the camera caught horses in mid-gallop, it was normal for them to be painted with the forequarters stretched in front and the hindquarters stretched out at the back. This was later found to be quite incorrect. Stubbs had already realized from his very close study of anatomy (some of his drawings of horse musculature are still used in veterinary text-books, so accurate and complete are they) that horses, when galloping, move their legs in a rotary cycle which never allowed for the 'stretched' position conventionally painted. When Edouard Muybridge set up his long line of cameras to analyse movement more scientifically, his pictures of a galloping horse proved Stubbs to be right.

Perspective may shorten or stretch form, but must always convince the viewer that it is his viewpoint which causes these distortions and not the drawing of the subject itself which is inaccurate or wrong.

In conclusion, we have four main categories, plus movement and perspective which stem from them, to give us dependable guidelines when drawing or painting animals, and these are considered over the following twelve pages. Actual measurements are not essential, but relative sizes – that is, the proportions of one creature compared with another, or the size or weight of an animal's limbs in context with its body – are important. You must use your eyes!

The skeleton of the squirrel (**fig. 11**) is dominated by the backbone, which is massively built and exceptionally supple. It extends into the bones of the tail at the pelvis, and attaches to the skull at the atlas and axis vertebrae. This line from skull to tail tip describes the essential profile of the creature. The heavy bones of the hind legs articulate in such a way as to fold the legs away under the creature's body, leaving only the feet and toes showing. As the body moves there are key points where bones make changes on the skin surface. Knees, elbows, jaw-line, all the heavy black lines shown in **fig. 12**, are pressure points and dictate form for any given attitude the squirrel adopts. Drawing these charming animals in your local park will give you a wealth of positions and attitudes, but you will need a comprehensive knowledge of the underlying structures when you come to translate your sketches into a finished piece of work, where you may well wish to adapt and alter your preliminary drawings to get your composition exactly as you want it. The skeleton of the squirrel is fairly typical of the skeletons of most small mammals, so a working knowledge of it can be applied to other similar creatures.

Finally, if you reduce the skeleton to its major parts you will see that the head and ribcage can be drawn as two spheres, one (the head) two-thirds the size of the other. A connecting line runs from the head, over the top of the ribs, and on to the tail tip. Halfway down this line the hind legs can be drawn in as an S-shaped line and the fore legs are placed at the front end of the ribs. Drawing the long line of the backbone and tail will give you the posture: compressed for a crouching animal, flattened for the beast in flight, etc. The limbs and the bulk of the torso will always fit into place once this line has been established and, using field observation and your notebook, you will be able to place your subject in exactly the attitude you want.

Fig. 12 The points of mobility on the animal's surface

STUDYING YOUR SUBJECT

For anyone who walks regularly in the countryside, or in a local park, specimens from nature will often be found. Dead birds or mammals may seem unsavoury, but quick inspection (for the not too squeamish) will decide you as to their suitability for bringing back to your work-place for closer study. Natural specimens are invaluable for the wealth of detail they allow you to commit to paper. The process of drawing from life (or death in this case) has two prime functions: as you work carefully with pencil and paper, you are not only building your library of reference with an accumulating collection of drawings, you are fixing in your mind the detail which, taken as a whole, gives authenticity to your work. There is a third function also, less important perhaps but still contributing to the quality of your painting. As you move your specimen bird or mammal about, changing its position for sketching, you will begin to get a feeling of the creature's articulation: the way it moves. How far, for example, can a bird's wing stretch forward and then back? How do the toes of a mouse move from being wide-spread to closed? All these details – all this knowledge – are there in the background whenever you come to apply paint to paper or canvas.

As you get to know your subjects, you can set them up with pins or blocks in more lifelike positions. You will have to 'cheat' your drawing in many small ways so as to completely reinvest your subject with life. Incidentally, one word of warning about using an eraser. If you make a mistake and rub it out, you will almost certainly make the same mistake again. Leave all the lines in until you get the right one, then, if you must, erase carefully, reinforcing the correct line with pencil as you go. I prefer drawings with all the lines the artist makes intact. Augustus John's study of a whippet, with its vague profile made up of many exploratory lines, becomes not only a perfect work of reference, but so precisely captures the nervous tension of the dog as to elevate it to a true work of art.

Try pushing your model (I shall refer to whatever little corpses you may have collected as 'models' from now on) into a position where you have one side

stretched and one side closed. In the case of the rat shown here, I positioned it in a typical pose using props and blocks and began a series of detailed drawings around one good general view of the complete animal. Sketch in with bold, simple lines the major areas of bulk in your model. Connect these with a profile (the line that you would draw if you were making a silhouette) which suggests tension. The hard, straight lines connecting curves suggest taut muscle, while depressed curves indicate slack. Now study your model for different textures. The sleek fur of the rat's back is shiny smooth, but the fluffy fur on the underparts appears dusty and diffused. Wet fur is spikey. With a brush, draw in a little of each. Now take a look at the detail of the rat's head. See how the fur there becomes finer in places until it disappears smoothly into the skin; see where follicles (the points on the skin where whiskers sprout) are placed. Study your own model and carefully draw in, with brush strokes which follow the direction of the hair, the contours around the small muscles of the face. These are crucial to animal painting as they give your subject facial expression. Make a special detail of the eye, opened wide, and note colour and size, for accuracy. Make details of the feet and fingers, and all the time you work, look at your model and then at your drawing for short, alternating periods. Draw a little, check a little, draw again, check again. Do not concentrate on one small area for too long at once, but jump from tail to ear, foot to eye, overall mass to detail of fingernail. Break off every few minutes, relax your concentration and look at something fresh for a few moments. Then go back to your drawing and your model with a new eye, and look at both for a while before starting to draw again. A discipline will develop which will be invaluable as a base for all your painting, as it has been for artists of all kinds since painting began. When you have studied your model and, with pencil, pen or brush, captured all its secrets on paper, change its position and start again. You cannot do enough, and after thirty years of painting wildlife, I still cannot do enough drawing from life.

Fig. 13 Doe rat: the approach, in watercolour, to a studio
specimen set up on blocks

FORM, PROPORTION AND PATTERN

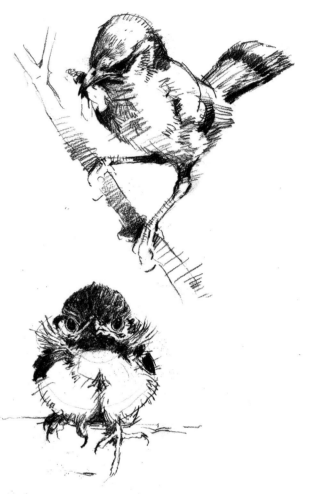

Fig. 14 Finch: opposing angles indicate aggression

Fig. 15 Fledgling: inter-relating lines indicate a passive attitude

When you begin sketching wildlife you will observe that the form of your animal subjects can be quickly pencilled in as a series of simple geometric shapes, rectangles, triangles and circles. The way in which form and proportion help express an animal's mood can also be suggested initially using this visual shorthand. Lines of tension are not usually drawn in, but with the drawing of the finch (**fig. 14**) I have shown the major lines to demonstrate that strongly opposing angles provide an aggressive expression, whereas compact and inter-relating lines, as with the fledgling (**fig. 15**), give a soft appearance. The relationships between the masses, illustrated in the drawing of the bank vole (**fig. 17**), enhance the creature's essential character.

The profile or outline of an animal will suggest that animal's attitude. An angular, taut silhouette will speak of tension and anger. Hunched shoulders and open mouths suggest threat or warning; a head turned sharply at right-angles to the body suggests fear. A soft, rounded, solid profile suggests content and calm.

Within the profile (the outline), there are surface patterns and surface textures. These behave in very specific ways as they follow the curves and contours of an animal's body, and some study will show you how. A strongly marked creature, like the serval (**fig. 16**), provides us, most obviously, with an example of how patterns alter and flatten as they follow a curved surface. A circle begins to distort as it turns away from the viewer, forming narrower and narrower elipses until, at the periphery of the curve (that point which approximates to the horizon on land), it appears as a straight line. Flat colour can be seen as a most subtle arrangement of mounds and curves simply by manipulating the superficial patterns.

The bank vole (**fig. 17**) is a triangle of simple forms when its bulk is analysed. It has no continuous patterning with which to suggest contour but its surface texture can be used in a similar way. The pattern made by fur as it curves away from the light source and ends in shadow can be readily used to indicate three dimensions.

86

Fig. 16 Serval: surface patterns reinforce contours and bulk

Fig. 17 Bank vole: analysing major forms in simple shapes

The beautiful, tapestry-like markings on many snakes and lizards (**fig. 18**) are a perfect challenge for the wildlife artist. I like to use individual dots of colour, oils or watercolour, to build up the effect, exactly as the animal is made up in real life. I allow this paint to dry and then overpaint with a semi-transparent dark, a shadow-colour, still applying the pigment dot by dot. The build-up of colour achieved in this way is much more intense and enamel-like; just as a reptile should be.

Fig. 18 Lizard: the use of surface patterns to enhance form and proportion

MOVEMENT

All animals have a gait which is peculiar to them alone: the stoat's snake-like scurry punctuated with sudden periscopic pauses; the loping, almost lazy bound of the hare; the quick trot of the fox. You must represent these accurately for each breed if your finished work is to be of any authority.

Looking at the drawings of the deer opposite (**figs. 19–21**), you can see the quite different forms that extended or contracted muscles make in the process of action. Once you have established the attitude of your subject, you must make sure that the musculature is modelled in the correct way for the pose. As a general rule, bent limbs carry bunched or knotted muscles which will be clearly defined by highlight and shadow; an overall rounded feeling should be aimed

for. Straight or stretched limbs look sleek and flat, and muscle shapes should be smooth and fluid, running together without much shadow contrast. The stag descending (**fig. 19**) has all the body weight on the front legs and is using muscle control to maintain an awkward position. In **fig. 20** the reverse of the above is true. Because of the extreme nature of the animal's situation, the muscles are bunched and clearly defined although the limbs are straight. This helps to strengthen the mood of the work and suggests tension in the composition. As with all detail, accuracy is essential if it is to lend any authority to the portrayal. Throughout the history of animal art, the paintings which have sought out the essential rather than the superficial have been of most lasting success.

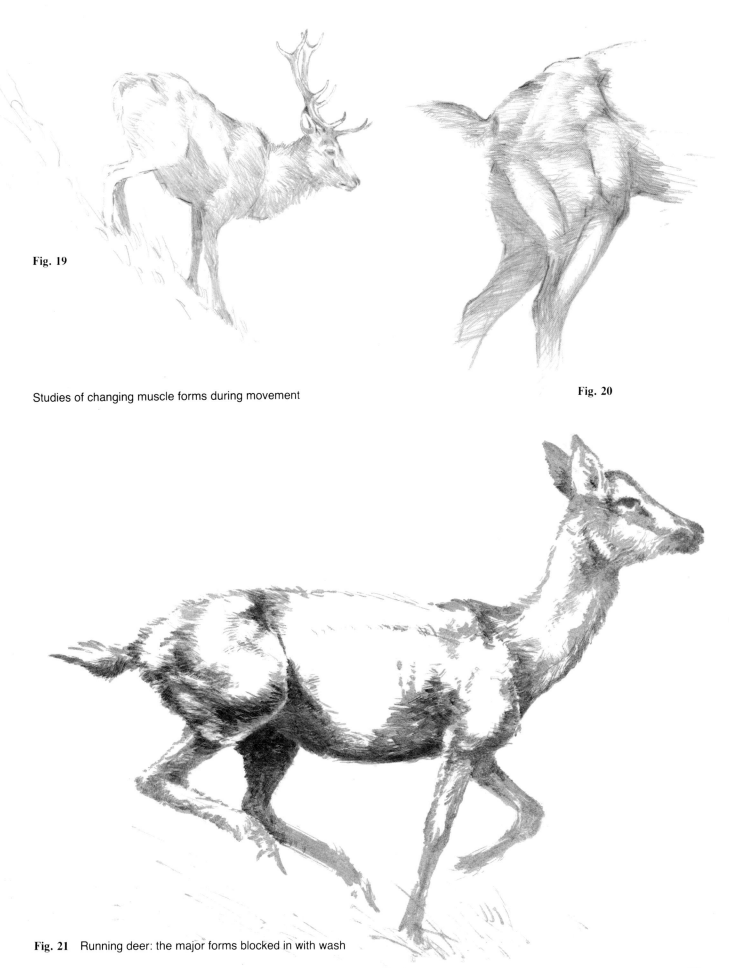

Fig. 19

Studies of changing muscle forms during movement

Fig. 20

Fig. 21 Running deer: the major forms blocked in with wash

89

ANATOMY OF FISH

The underlying skeleton of a fish describes its proportions, its form and its action in a precise and inviolate way. The soft, flexible areas such as the belly and throat are supported by the ribs and skull without having any rigidity from bones passing through them. They are, therefore, of variable shape and size and, if twisted or folded, will show creases on the skin surface. The back (dorsal) and tail (caudal) muscles are heavily boned with fine interlocking spines originating at the vertebrae and curving out and back through these tissues. The skull is a solid shell of bone, very near the surface and allowing no flexibility whatsoever.

Once the anatomy here (**fig. 22**) is clearly understood, and the exterior detailing of a given species (in this case a common carp) is noted accurately, you should be able to draw your fish from any angle and in any shape you wish. Reduce your subject to a few essential lines and you have your proportions (**fig. 23**). Add shading and tone and you achieve form (**fig. 24**). So, if you want to show your fish leaping and twisting, know your skeleton. I think one of the nicest ways to study a fish's bone structure is as you carefully separate it from the flesh on a dinner plate; but if you can get hold of a fish, or if you can get to a museum where you can take a sketchbook, a 5 mm HB automatic pencil and a kneadable rubber and see one on display, then a careful drawing will do more for your knowledge of animal structure than twenty written works. Be very strict with yourself, however, and get your drawing *absolutely* correct, counting the bones and getting the number right, the proportions accurate, and the angles, most importantly, showing the natural line that the overlay of muscles will take when you come to paint or draw a less studied subject.

Like a beautiful engine or a great building, the exterior is arrived at only after a real awareness of the underlying structure and a knowledge of the insides are achieved. While these 'foundations' are unseen, and often unappreciated, yet their absence or an inadequate understanding of their function leaves the finished work lacking in authority and, somehow, unsatisfactory to the viewer.

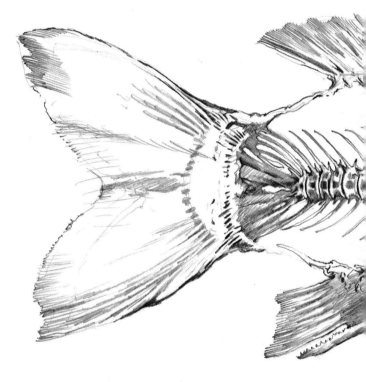

Fig. 22 Common carp: the underlying frame

Fig. 23 Basic proportions

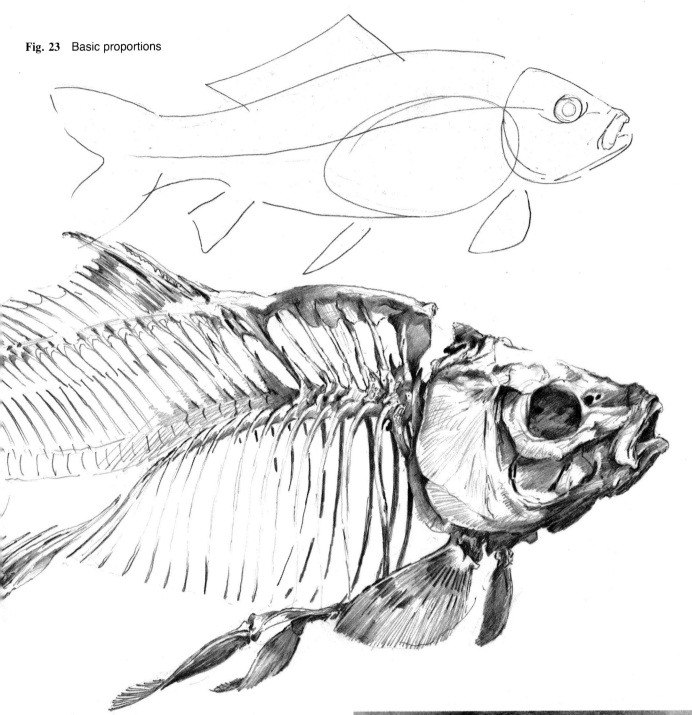

Fig. 24 The textures, tones and forms which clothe the skeleton

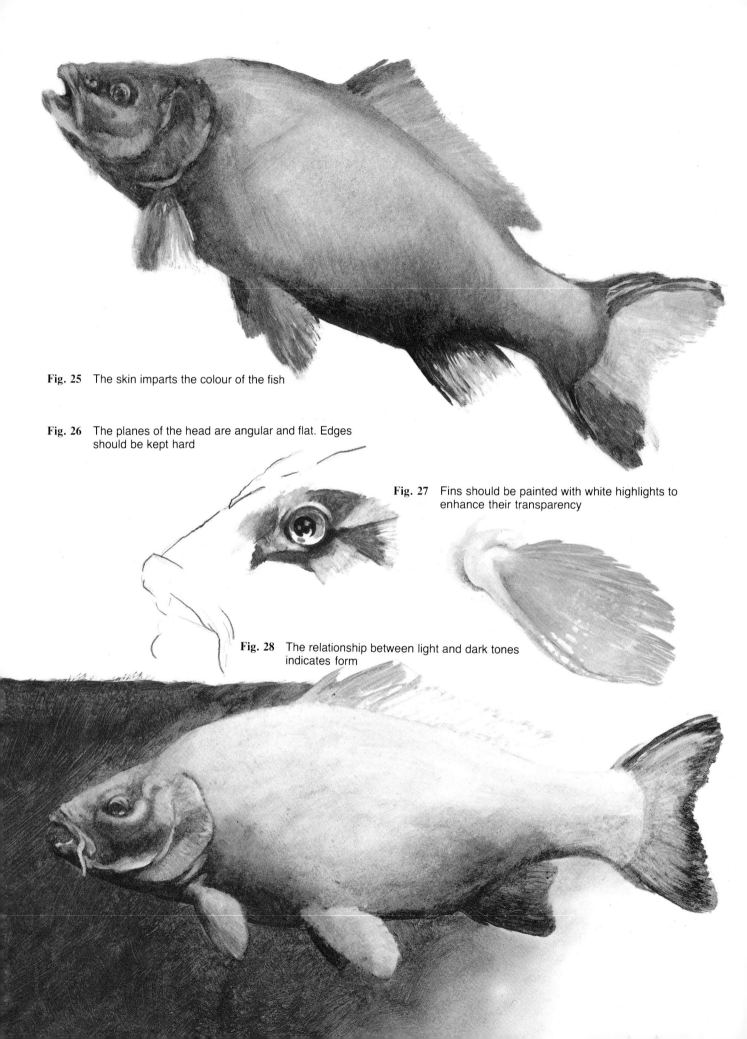

Fig. 25 The skin imparts the colour of the fish

Fig. 26 The planes of the head are angular and flat. Edges should be kept hard

Fig. 27 Fins should be painted with white highlights to enhance their transparency

Fig. 28 The relationship between light and dark tones indicates form

STUDYING YOUR SUBJECT

When approaching the subject of your picture and contemplating the technique most suitable and the process of painting, it is often of help to consider the actual structure of your creature. Under the scales of a fish there is a leathery, smooth skin, and it is this which imparts the colour (**fig. 25**) – the scales are transparent in the main, and have a speckled, reflective edge. The contours of the fish, and their reaction to the light source, describe the animal's form (**fig. 28**). There we are: three parts of the fish, easily reproduced, one on top of the other, in paint.

Using oils or watercolour, begin with the forms in a dark colour on white. Overlay the general colour of the fish, keeping the lighter parts of the form crisp and clean, and merging your colour into the background darks where you cover shading. Overpaint the scales, one at a time, in long, lateral rows, reflecting the general colour, and painting white (you can lay this on in a solid mass) for the underparts. This gives you surface texture and pattern, and the undulations of the rows reinforce the form, the 'roundness' of your fish. Paint any pattern the fish carries as you would build up a mosaic: use small dots of colour as 'tessare' (the individual pieces of coloured material which make up a mosaic). Your fish should now be finished, save for highlights. Any wet, slippery object will throw off pure white highlights – study the fishmonger's slab! The whole can appear a little crude, however, and it is necessary to smooth layers of overpainting into each other with a fan brush, say a Dalon Series D.55 No. 3, to achieve subtlety and realism.

Fig. 29 The technique of painting scales

Fig. 30 Fish float! A strong shadow lifts your subject away from its surroundings

ANATOMY OF BIRDS IN FLIGHT

The curvature of a bird's wings depends on the flying (down) stroke, or the retrieving (up) stroke. A bird gains lift and forward flying speed by pushing down hard with both wings and dipping down, slightly, by using the tail. If you paint a bird coming in to land, it would look wrong seen on a down stroke, the stroke of acceleration. Similarly, if you paint a bird taking off, it would look wrong seen on an up stroke, the stroke of deceleration or braking. Think carefully of the circumstances you place your subject in and get the details right.

The striking owl (**fig. 31**) is seen in an extreme position, at the peak of physical effort and concentration. A look at the skeleton (**fig. 32**) will show you that these remarkable contortions in no way disobey the laws and conditions of the creature's anatomy, indicating just how articulated a wild animal's structure can be. Within an accurate framework underlying the finished form, there is ample opportunity to find images or compositions of remarkable impact.

94

Fig. 31

Fig. 32 Owl: a thorough study of the skeleton will give you confidence when handling extreme action

FIELD NOTES

Fig. 33 Sparrowhawk: identification sketch

Fig. 34 · First rough sketch of the scene

Much preparatory work can be done at home before you venture out into the field with pencil and sketchbook. I know of a sparrowhawk's nest locally, and decided to make use of the site for a picture. Before I went out, I drew an outline of the bird (copied roughly from a bird identification book such as *Collins Field Guide to British Birds*) in strong, simple lines (**fig. 33**). I would fill this in with more precise detail in the field. Then I sketched a rough outline of the composition I wanted and headed separate sheets of my sketchbook with the necessary components: nest, foliage, sky, branches – every detail that might enhance my composition had a page to itself.

Once in the field, and hidden beneath the sparrowhawk's nest, I positioned my equipment around me so as to keep movement to a minimum. The first drawing was a general view of the nest and surroundings and, very lucky this time, the male sparrowhawk (musket) alighting several times to feed his brooding mate (**fig. 34**). I flipped back the pages of my sketchbook to write in some plumage details on my ready-drawn dummy. As one observes a site like this for a period of time, one begins to identify the eccentric or the unusual in one's field of view. Here, the hawks had included the red and white cardboard of a cigarette packet in the structure of the nest, and it struck an incongruous note – a device which might well work in a picture to highlight the subject. All these details should be drawn and described.

Always remember to keep a weather eye on good background material for your paintings: bark, rock, earth banks with roots, plants, branches, posts, gates,

water margins, nests – the list is endless. Keep notes on colour and collect samples of leaves, twigs, and the like, from your background scene, to give you a base colour guide. Also record the creatures you might expect to see in any environment you consider worth noting, and look around for actual signs of the wildlife which has frequented your site. The more knowledge you acquire, the better your work will be. When you feel happy with the amount of field work done, return to your studio and start cross-referencing with photographs of your subject from books and natural-history magazines, and build up a set of detail drawings which describe any aspect of your picture which demands absolute accuracy (**fig. 35**).

By now you should have a very clear picture in your mind of what your finished piece will look like. Make a drawing, to size, of your composition and include, in as much detail as possible, all the elements you have gathered from your field trips and your research (**fig. 36**). It is now that you will uncover any weakness in your composition and can begin 'honing' or 'fining' your picture: rounding out the work with supporting detail; altering the attitude of your subject a little here, a little there; sharpening the look of the thing so as to get the maximum effect from your images.

A sequence from field to finished drawing in the studio allows you time and practice to get to the heart of your subject. As you work on you will familiarize yourself with all aspects of your picture, and by the time you come to put paint on paper or canvas you should know, in every particular, the drawing, the composition, the sequence of painting and the degree of finish that you require to achieve your goal.

Fig. 35 Detail drawings

Fig. 36 Finished studio rough

STUDY OF FEATHERS

This classic study (in oils) for your reference library, detailing a bird's wing, will give you much more information than simply shape and colour. The relationships between colours can be projected on to the canvas as a guide to colour over the whole of your painting, and the proportions of bright detail to drab background can be ascertained and used as a guide for your work in general. The careful study of these details of nature in this way can give you valuable guidelines which you will be able to apply to all aspects of your art.

Pin up your model close to the work surface and sit down comfortably to study it. Look and concentrate for a while, getting a general feel of the overall colours, and then decide how you can achieve an accurate result with the *least* number of tube colours possible, squeezing a small amount of each (about the size of a pea) on to the sides of your palette (**fig. 37**). Use a pencil brush (Dalon D.77 No. 3 or 4 is about right) and mix a light background colour to base your work. (If you feel unhappy about drawing

straight on to the paper with a brush, draw a faint outline with an HB fine point first.) Keep your paint thin and transparent and mix only with diluent (turps substitute or white spirit) – *no oil*! Let the brush make its own feather effect by pushing the paint around with flicks and short strokes, and let the brush hairs spread and separate. The colour should be no more than tinted spirit, very transparent (**fig. 37**). Work back from the wing tips with a dark colour (**fig. 38 and 39**), then overlay with a solid white to give the barred effect (**fig. 40**); let the colours blend at the edges on the paper. Fill in the dark patterns on the small underwing feathers and then paint up to them with white. Allow an hour for drying, then, using a very transparent brown with a *hint* of blue, brush in the shading with a small fan (**fig. 40**). If you notice colour coming off and mixing with your shadow colour, stop and leave to dry more. Finish with a small pencil brush (Dalon D.77 No. 1) by outlining and sharpening up details and edges where necessary. Wait two days, then fix with a matt spray.

Fig. 37

Fig. 38 First stage

Fig. 39 Second stage

Fig. 40 Finished stage

99

PAINTING BUTTERFLIES

Fig. 41 Field sketches

There are certain subjects which require a special approach and are very demanding of an artist's technique. Moths and butterflies are the most subtle and delicately marked of all insects, and their caterpillars are similarly patterned and shaded. Careful observation and plenty of drawings in your field notebook must come before you can approach butterfly painting (**fig. 41**). Study the way the wings appear from different angles and try to avoid the obvious symmetrical pose with both wings laid flat. Detail is essential with insects: make as many different drawings of detail as you can and make them quite large, say four times larger than life. The intricate structures should be carefully drawn with an HB pencil on white cartridge.

Their size presents a problem to begin with and, generally, I like to compose a picture including moths or butterflies by having a wide, drab backdrop with the insects as exquisite droplets of brilliant colour placed carefully within the picture plane but quite small and precise. The background needs research as most butterflies are specific to certain plants. It is a good idea to make notes on foliage and any other features in your subject's immediate surroundings.

Once you know your butterfly and the relevant foliage, paint in with a solid, dark tone, a background colour which complements your subject. The brightly coloured Vanessids (Red Admiral, Emperor, etc.) can take a strong range of good greens (**fig. 45**), but the Fritillaries or Meadow Browns would be overpowered by these and need a much more neutral tone; green-brown or amber-brown would enhance and heighten the impact of these tiny brown/red butterflies, and an underlying shadow will throw the subject into relief.

The patterns on the wings are made up of minute scales, each a distinct colour, and, if you can, you should reproduce these patterns similarly with paint (**fig. 42**). Painting two butterflies together gives you the opportunity to show the underwing as well as the dorsal colour, but always work from actual specimens when attempting this particular scene.

Caterpillars (**fig. 43**) must be accurately drawn and coloured, too, and should be identifiable as to type. Use an HB pencil to get detail and watercolour to make a side-view reference picture for your library. Look up the animal's proper name and label your painting with it.

Fig. 42 Swallowtail: detailed study of the wing colour and pattern

Fig. 43

Fig. 44 Try to avoid the obvious symmetrical pose

Fig. 45

COMPOSITION AND INTERPRETATION

Fig. 46 Rabbits and stoats: acquiring a reference library with pencil sketches in the field

I can give no better advice as you consider what to paint than to choose a subject you know. Painting a wildlife picture is, in part, a question of using your artistic skills to reveal something of nature which the viewer would otherwise not be privy to, and it is the responsibility of the artist not to misrepresent his subjects but to enhance and add to the viewer's awareness of them. It is difficult enough coping with the practical problems of technique without adding to the task. A subject you are familiar with will also give you confidence in drawing, painting and scale.

Suppose the scenario for your canvas is a stoat and a rabbit: an elusive scene that few can have witnessed at first hand. Which animal do you feature most

prominently? The rabbit, unsuspecting, browsing in the foreground, or the sinister stoat, an ominous shadow in the rear? Or do you paint the stoat almost filling the frame? Do you intertwine the two forms almost as a heraldic device, implying the more profound relationship of the two creatures in the wild? These are the kind of questions every artist must ask himself when planning a composition of this kind.

In this instance, I felt that the character of each animal should be delineated. The stoat I wished to appear lithe and ruthless, the arch predator, crouched and determined (perhaps with a glitter of white as the fangs appear behind the smile). The rabbit was more difficult; no longer warm and fecund, chewing dandelion or sorrel, enjoying the summer heat, but the quarry, hunted and caught, with an awareness of its part having been played and resignation in its eye. There was a vacancy of expression in the rabbit which I wanted to paint to complement and contrast with the glittering ferocity which the lip-licking stoat imparted (**fig. 47**).

Begin with sketchbook and pencil and start playing with shapes taken from your field notes, establishing scale between the principals (rabbits are bigger than stoats, but by how much?) and rhythm (**fig. 46**). If you cannot find a stoat in the field you may have to resort to photographs. Think of the light and dark of the backdrop as you position your subjects within the picture plane; think also of the most advantageous point of view – choose one that most helps the impact of your scene. Can your viewpoint be enhanced by a close-up? Do you want to contrast the lovely landscape with the teeth and claws? Think of yourself as an architect drawing up a groundplan before attempting to build the reality. I like to consider the subject of a picture as I might chance across it in the wild: a fleeting glimpse of an animal poised before flight. Such an image should be fixed as soon as possible in the sketch form with notes. Your painting should attempt to subdue the less important parts of the picture whilst spotlighting the most relevant details. I sometimes use a bright shaft of light in an otherwise shaded scene to leave absolutely no doubt as to the painting's focal point. This use of shadow and illumination is a very useful tool in the wildlife artist's range of techniques, considering the elusive nature of his subjects. Bearing in mind the overall tone of the piece, begin sketching in these darks and lights in your composition (**fig. 48**).

The background components can be reduced to textures and forms of an almost abstract nature at this point. Positive lines, such as branches or reeds, and negatives such as shadows or spaces, join together to form pointers or indicate direction. They are valuable devices for leading the view to the chosen centre of the composition, in this case the glitter in the stoat's eye. Establish bold lines. Do not be half-hearted about relationships. Do not allow forms to touch just at the edges as this is awkward, but keep them well apart or make them overlap strongly. Make two cut-out shapes representing the stoat and the rabbit and move them about until you discover the most readable and exciting position with curves and lines flowing. Move a leg here or a head there, if it helps; do not be limited to your original pose if it conflicts with its counterpart, however pleased you are with that shape in isolation. Rhythms should be achieved in tones of light and shade. The attitude of a creature when frozen in two dimensions must suggest the pace and vitality of the living animal; the stoat is lithe and fluid, the rabbit stolid and shy. There is always a place for deliberately rendering a subject out of character for the sake of tension, but be careful – like garlic in a good meal, use sparingly.

Fig. 47

Fig. 48 Pencil sketch of the composition

You are now ready to start painting. Clear a space for your reference material – photographs, specimens or whatever – and make sure your equipment is prepared. Having established the composition after experimenting with pencil and sketchbook, and deciding to work in oils, the major lines and shapes must be transferred to the canvas. I use one of two methods: I cover the back of my rough drawing with pencil shading (a Black Beauty is useful here), position the sketch on the canvas, and go over all the main lines and forms with an HB pencil. This draws through on to the painting surface rather like a carbon

Fig. 49 Establishing the light and dark tones

copy. The other method, for work that needs to be scaled up in size, is to draw a grid of squares over the rough sketch, then an equal number of squares of sufficient size to cover the canvas. Each small square on the sketch can be accurately redrawn in its corresponding large square on the painting surface. Once the rough is transferred, I like to fill out the layout with charcoal, concentrating on the main areas of light and shade. This would be wrong for watercolour as the charcoal would dirty the subtle washes, but oil assimilates charcoal quite readily.

The overall colour of **fig. 49** is a green-brown, so I mixed a dark tone with Vandyke Brown and Prussian Blue and started painting in the shaded areas with a Dalon D.22 ½ inch flat. When this was complete, I stood back to see, for the first time, the composition as a whole. It was at this point that I started changing a line here or a shape there, beginning to fine the work as I went along. Never be strict about following original lines; it is not until the brush begins to bring out the images on the canvas that weaknesses can be remedied or additions made for improvement. Be flexible and prepared to change and adapt as your work progresses.

105

I worked into the picture while the shadow colour was still retrievable to blend colour and texture into shadow. (Although apparently dry, the paint was still soft enough to be made fluid again when brushed with turpentine. The more linseed oil in the original colour mix, the longer it will stay 'retrievable'.) The painting was now at the stage shown outside the central square, with detail beginning to emerge and colour being enhanced (**fig. 50**). In some parts of the background this soft focus and vague detail was as far as I would go, preferring to save the high finish and strong detail for the important central area of the picture.

The stoat and the rabbit's head, and the way that these two intertwine, make a clear statement about the creatures and their relationship in the wild. The pose is the traditional one for victor and vanquished and this area of the painting contains the essence of the work, so I concentrated the strongest painting here. I brushed in the shaded fur with a Dalon D.66 No. 1, teasing out the earlier shadow colour and blending the two. Into the wet paint of the shadow fur I painted the lighter shades until I was painting almost white fur in strong illumination. These areas were blended into one another so as to give an even transposition from dark to light.

The face of the stoat is the very centre of the piece and was painted with most strength. I painted in the overall rust colour first, then into this colour placed the eye and the inside of the mouth with Lamp Black, straight from the tube. The white fur was painted on so as to use the dark underpainting as shading and modelling for the features; by painting white on with a single stroke it remained clean white, but by using more than one stroke and pushing the paint about, the undercolour started coming to the surface and 'shaded' the white. The resulting tones give a remarkably accurate rendering of fur and perfectly describe the creature's facial expression. The fine hairs on the muzzle and brows were made by scratching with a compass point; a finer and sharper effect than a paintbrush could achieve. The highlights in the eye are Titanium White straight from the tube, dotted in with the point of a Dalon D.77 No. 000.

At this stage I looked at the work as a finished piece; as a whole. I reinforced the shading around the subjects so as to bring them well forward, and worked on odd details of grass, background and subject until I was satisfied that I needed to go no further. The work was put away flat and left to dry thoroughly. After a week or two, I signed the picture and varnished it.

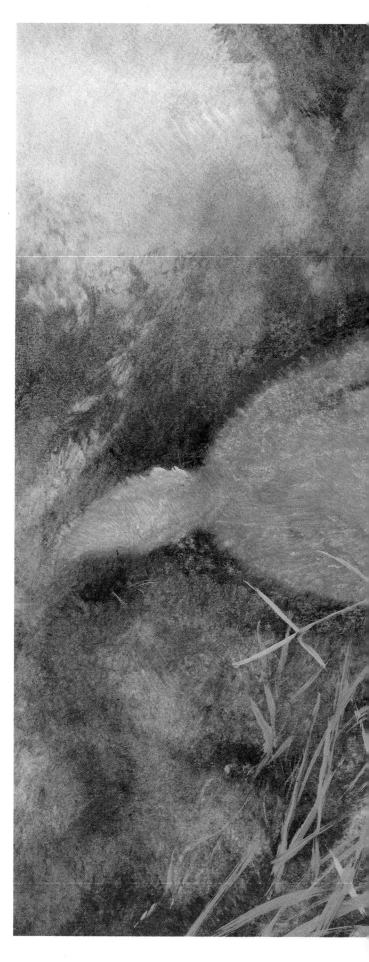

Fig. 50 Developing colour, texture and detail

106

DRAWING IN THE FIELD

Certain circumstances will not allow you merely to sketch in pencil or charcoal and then return to your studio to work up your painting to a finish. Sometimes you will need more studied observation on site. The trout stream is a classic example. Fish appear fleetingly, if at all, and can only really be drawn from memory. When dealing with a subject like this, stand and watch for as long as you can – patience here can be worth more than its own reward. Build up a mental picture of your fish, as you watch them, and look for regular or recurring patterns of action. A rising trout comes straight to the surface then curves into a U shape to dart back to the bottom. Fish holding their position in a current, wriggle constantly in a shallow S shape, while fish holding their position in still water, stay very straight, using only the movement of their fins. While these images and observations are fresh in your mind, try putting them down on paper (**fig. 51**). Pencil in essential lines quickly and in one stroke (the line from the fish's nose, down the centre of the back to the tail, is the only one you need worry about here), attempting the fluid movement of the creature itself. Draw in possible positions of fins. If your sketches are unsatisfactory to start with, stop drawing and start

looking again. Eventually you will have a few pages of fish in all manner of poses. Even if you do not have the fish there that you need for your painting, by now you will know so well how these creatures move that you will be able to draw it from memory.

The water, water-weeds and banks are permanent fixtures, yet a pencil sketch can rarely carry enough information about such a scene, so an oil sketch, done on the spot, is needed. For this, use a flat, smooth-surfaced card (Bristol board is good) cut to a convenient size to carry (A4). Card absorbs oil and spirit quite quickly and your sketch will dry nicely before packing to carry home. The use of a brush handle or a bamboo scraping tool is much more effective on a smooth surface and much of your sketching will be of this type; brushing on solid areas of colour and then scraping back to the natural white surface beneath. Be quick and bold as you work. It is the impression you wish to capture, not the detail. Look and look again as you work.

Make sure you establish the main areas of light and dark, and begin to distinguish between below and above the water surface. Try to capture the distortions that an irregular water surface imparts to solid

Fig. 51   Trout: the field sketch in charcoal pencil

Fig. 52 First stage

Fig. 53 Second stage

Fig. 54 Finished stage

objects seen beneath it. To do this successfully, make your brush behave like the water itself. Apply a dark colour, representing the overall tone and hue of the water, and with a scribe or scoring tool scrape the forms of the weeds into the wet paint (the dark colour may need lubricating with a little linseed oil, once or twice, to keep it from drying out), building up a general impression of the masses and forms made by the water-flow on the weedbed (**fig. 52**). Using a dry fan brush, Dalon D.55 No. 2, draw a series of zig-zag strokes across the line of the weeds, which will reproduce the effect of ripples by distorting the lines of the weeds. With a small pencil brush, Dalon D.77 No. 1, loaded with a pale green, wriggle in the colour of the weeds, following the distorted lines of the fan-brushed base colour. Follow this procedure over the whole of the picture area, continually stopping to blur edges and distress and distort hard lines with your No. 2 fan (**fig. 53**). In my sketch I made the rising trout the focal point and I wanted the radiating rings of water from this rise to enhance the fish like a halo. I scraped the series of elipses (circles seen in perspective) with my brush handle and softened them with the No. 2 fan.

Now for the fish themselves (**fig. 54**). There is a problem with painting fish. The light shines on them from above, where they are dark coloured, and they are in shadow on the underside, where they are light coloured. So, we must paint the white in shadow and the dark illuminated. Observation of fish in water is the only answer to this problem, and you will soon see that, in certain lights and at certain angles, the fish can be lighter above than below. In my sketch, however, with a point of view from fairly high above, the relationship of light and shade to colour is dark above and lighter below, as one would expect. Paint in your light colour, then the dark, merge the two colours with a Dalon D.88 $\frac{1}{4}$ inch, then dot in the pattern on the flanks of the fish. Blur and soften by flicking your No. 2 fan over the whole surface, and repoint (make sharp and clear again) any areas that you feel need precision and clarity, such as the heads of the fish. Dot in highlights with Titanium White lifted straight from the tube and soften these by fanning the wet paint diagonally left top to right bottom, then left bottom to right top. Keep a light touch and a free-moving hand working from the wrist.

This sketch took me less than ten minutes at the riverbank and all the materials were carried in a small box easily contained in a satchel. The paper was Bristol board mounted on offcuts of corrugated card (cut from the clean, flat sides of cardboard boxes) with an aerosol adhesive. The end result, in conjunction with photographs of weed and water detail, and text-book references for the fish, contained everything that I needed before starting on a finished work back in the studio.

THE DEGREE OF FINISH

Many people see wildlife painting only as very highly finished and photographically realistic. However, sketchy impressions can often convey much more precisely the nature or form of your subject and, after all, wild creatures are usually seen only as a series of fleeting images conveying an 'impression' of form rather than a clear description. Any artist will tell you that one of the most useful skills you can develop is the ability to recognize when your piece of work is finished – knowing when to stop. When I say finished, I must underline that I do not necessarily use the word in the sense of everything being complete; a few quick lines describing a running fox can be 'finished' as a picture. When a painting says everything you wish it to say about your subject, any further painting is merely embroidery and will only distract the viewer.

The picture of an otter was started with a conté pencil drawing (**fig. 55**) taken to a fairly high degree of detail. Colour washes in oils or watercolour were then applied, beginning the process of building up colour in layers. Darker colours, as for the deep water behind the lily pads, were strengthened with heavier washes until the desired degree of opacity (the 'solidness' of a colour) was achieved (**fig. 56**). The form of the animal was flashed in with ragged strokes, using a dark shading colour and a medium round-ended brush, and these were blended into the background with a fan brush to give the indistinct, underwater feel. The lily pads were given detail – ribs and shading – with a No. 2 or 3 round-ended brush. Highlights were sketched in (**fig. 57**), and as I was dealing with moving water, the brush (in this case a fairly large pencil brush) had to be kept loose and fluid. The difference between fur under water and above it had to be made clear (this defines the plane of the water surface as well) and colour was the simplest method of achieving this. The final section (**fig. 58**) shows high finish. The diffused highlights in the foreground were painted by 'pointing' – thick dots of pure white were put on the canvas and then 'flared' with a small fan brush whisked gently back and forth across the points of white along both diagonals. The fur about the otter's face was painted with a fine pencil brush (No. 0), applying the colour in strokes along the lie of the pelt and shading to bring out the forms of the face. The eyes were clearly delineated and the highlights put in, using pure white. The painting was complete.

However, whether the last stage (**fig. 58**) – or come to that, **fig. 56.** or **fig. 57** – although highly finished, says any more about otters than the original conté drawing (**fig. 55**) is debatable. I suspect not.

Fig. 55   First stage

Fig. 56 Second stage   **Fig. 57** Third stage   **Fig. 58** Finished stage

SHORELINE SNIPE

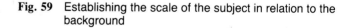

Fig. 59 Establishing the scale of the subject in relation to the background

Now you have had some practice at drawing specimens at your table, you will be able to collect field notes in preparation for a finished work. Let us go step by step through the process of translating a scene into an oil painting.

The scene will probably have suggested itself as the basis of a picture if you are familiar with it (stick to what you know!) either because of a sudden change of light or, as in the case of the seashore scene here, the arrival into a known landscape of some unusual visitors. The flock of snipe stayed for several days and I studied them with binoculars for a day before going out with a pad and a 5 mm HB propelling pencil (always with a sharp point) to get some sketches.

Shapes and patterns as the birds fly in groups; details and notes – length of wing, bill, body, etc.; size and position relative to the horizon and tideline; atmosphere and lighting; notes on colour: all this information was needed (**figs. 59 and 60**). As you study to collect such information you are absorbing the overall feeling of the place. Written notes are just as useful as drawings, and if you have a watercolour box, paint a spectrum that sums up the colour of the scene. In my painting (**fig. 61**), amber, grey-green and brown, with peripheral splashes of blue and reflected white light, were all I needed. Do not try to use every colour in your box in every picture you paint. Less can very often be more.

Fig. 60 Preliminary field sketches

Fig. 61 Establishing the colour scheme

113

Back in the studio, after toying with a sketchbook of white cartridge and a 6B pencil and trying out different views, I had a fairly clear idea that my picture would be a clear, brightly lit, but slightly wintry seascape, with my snipe, like a litter of windblown autumn leaves, cascading across it as they coast down to land. I wanted to capture the overall pattern of their flight, rather than detail, so I could light them strongly – some almost silhouettes – as if by a high sun. This was also very dramatic and provided a strong, dark pattern against a soft, pale ground. The birds cut very positively across the strong horizontals made by the sea. A soft reflective feel to the sand made the whole background very watery, also in contrast to the snipe.

I quickly sketched in the birds, and when the flock was right – the right number and weight – I tried on a piece of tracing paper various possibilities for the horizon and tideline. When satisfied, I marked them in on the watercolour and began painting (**fig. 62**). I painted in the sea, the sand and the sky with thin washes, building up to the intensity I wanted, using a generous sable ($\frac{1}{2}$ inch). As the pencil lines would show through I could paint right across the picture – I did not try to paint round the birds. Then, with a No. 1 pencil brush I sketched in the shadows in brown, and when correct in strength, I used just a wet brush to tease the brown out over the remaining areas of the birds. I was now familiar with my composition to the point where my finished oil painting could be executed with an absolutely clear idea as to the order of work, the colours involved and any alterations or corrections that might be required. I had also eliminated the awful business of staring at a completely blank canvas with a brain to match. An image needs time to settle, especially for the person responsible for creating it, so I gave myself some time to study the picture before I started on my canvas. I put it out of sight for a while then came back to it fresh. I sometimes look at my work reflected in a mirror – you will be surprised how fresh your view of a piece of work can be by using this trick.

Fig. 62   Watercolour studio sketch

I like to transfer a very precise composition like *Shoreline Snipe* in a very precise way. Tracing the major lines and marks off the watercolour, I began to redraw them on to canvas primed with gesso (a creamy plaster giving a smooth, paperlike surface), using a 2H pencil and carbon paper. The sky was painted in one 'pass', using the watercolour pinned to the board to the left of the canvas for reference. I mixed colour as near to the watercolour as possible then put it on the canvas with a Dalon ½ inch flat. Texture and inconsistent paint density came automatically as the brush worked across the gesso. I blended out those textures which I did not want with a Dalon No. 6 fan but some enhanced my painting beautifully and these I kept in – always look out for the 'happy accident'! I used a maul-stick 1 metre (1 yd) long to help me rule in the horizon across the canvas with a Dalon No. 3 flat, and then painted the sea from this point down. Remember that distance softens colour; I painted with increasing intensity as I came towards the tideline. I left the waves until the sand was painted in. By using colours from the sky, I could achieve a reflective surface on the sand (always softening and blending with a fan) and the desired wetness. The waves were painted with pure white, one side being left hard, the other blended out. A touch of shadow between the leading edge of the waves and the wet sand seated the water firmly on top of the land, where it belonged.

By this time, only the birds remained. An exact copy of my practice with the watercolour sketch, building up to just the right strength and opacity, achieved the correct result, and by being careful to paint all overlapping forms in the correct order, I completed the painting (**fig. 63**). If any areas of a finished picture seem harsh or raw, wait until the paint is just going off and then dust all over with a large fan, making doubly sure that it is dust-free and clean. Then, only a signature is lacking.

Fig. 63 *Shoreline Snipe*: finished oil

SHORELINE SNIPE

GALLERY:
OBSERVATIONS AND DETAILS

Fig. 64 *Heron*

The pictures here are all works which were commissioned or painted to a commercial brief, for publishers or industry. They have a superficial similarity, being the work of one artist, yet each one makes a special point and represents the solution to a different problem.

I have described each picture bearing in mind its one special facet, whether that be the technique of painting, unusual composition, or unexpected point of view. A painting can, and perhaps should, contain all of these points, yet these pictures have been selected because each one is an example of how one particular problem was solved. They were all achieved using the methods and techniques described in the preceding chapters, and where details are illustrated they are shown at actual size.

The heron (**fig. 64**) is a creature hardly ever seen at close quarters. This leaves the artist with two possibilities: to represent the bird in a natural way and paint it as it would naturally be seen; or to give the viewer the benefit of the artist's ability to get behind the scenes or into otherwise closed places. I felt that this bird was distinctive enough not to get lost in the wider view, and I consequently saw it as part of a much larger landscape. The three main elements – bird, tree and background – are each quite distinct in texture and act as foils, one against the others. Another important consideration to be taken into account is the size of the bird: big enough to carry some degree of detail (especially about the head), yet small enough within the picture plan to seem hidden and secret.

The bee-eater (**fig. 65**) is not only exotic in colour and form, but in life-style. No background was necessary in this painting except for a suitable overall drab to offset the jewel-like quality of the bird, so I painted an earth bank, grey in general colour and featureless save for a strong diagonal to 'raise' the bird off the canvas. The hole in the bank, obvious home of the bees, gives a reason for the action taking place. The bird was painted in flat colours as this is how the creature would be seen flitting by. One wing was left unpainted: the 'happy accident' which lent some life to an otherwise stiff watercolour composition.

The detail of the bee (**fig. 66**) shows another example of the 'happy accident'. I tried painting the flashing wings of the flying insect several times and found it most difficult to resolve properly. I decided to erase what I had painted with a little water and begin again. I removed the water with my finger and discovered that the smudgy fingerprint, with a flash of white paper showing through, was just the effect I wanted.

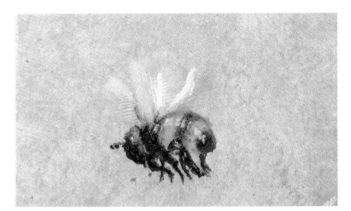

Fig. 66

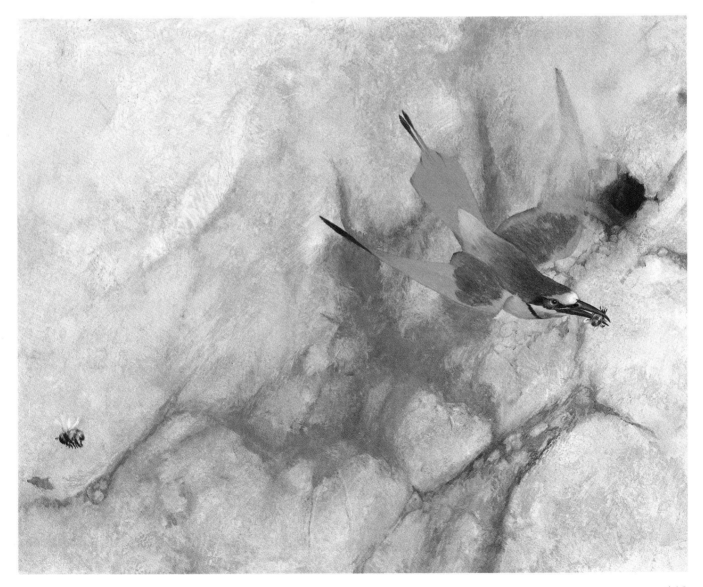

Fig. 65 *Bee-eater*

This painting (**fig. 67**), from Conoco's 1985 calendar, presented me with a particularly unusual problem. As a subject for a wildlife painting, the toad, I must admit, would not spring immediately to mind. Being one of the twelve required 'hunter and hunted' subjects, however, it was necessary to look closely at the animal and to discover some aspect of it which was aesthetically acceptable. This proved harder than I expected and I was beginning to despair of the piece when one of those 'happy accidents' occurred and the picture was set: I was gardening, and a toad walked slowly into the sunlight from under a clump of dock and posed most professionally at my feet; the play of light on the warty skin and the flecks of orange fire in its eyes turned the creature into a thing of jade and amber, quite perfect! I had already assembled details of toads from photographs and earlier drawings, so I had only to carry this image in my mind's eye and bring it to the studio.

I started this oil painting by laying Vandyke Brown on the paper with a Dalon 1 inch flat and working shapes into it with a wooden scraper and a rag, all the time keeping the paint fluid, filling in bits which did not work, and holding those which did. The underlying texture of leaf mould and dead twigs achieved in this way has a most convincing form. Then I began to paint in shadows here and there, with a Dalon D.77 No. 5, to 'flesh out' this background, lending depth and creating visual interest. As you look at an overall texture like this, shapes will suddenly reveal themselves to you as leaves or pieces of bark or whatever, and a fleck of shadow and a dot or two to highlight an edge will reinforce these images and make them clear to everyone. Bring out these forms as they occur to you and slowly build up the strength and quality of your backgrounds. Do not let your painting be spread evenly over the picture plane but give the viewer 'high' points to focus on. These will lead the eye over the canvas in leaps and bounds and make the picture an exciting visual experience.

I used this technique here to lead the viewer into the painting and finally to the focal point, the head of the toad. I painted the leaves of the dock next, which were an extension of the background as far as painting technique went. They were, however, raised above the surface of the ground and had to appear so. Use of shadow is invaluable and should always be considered as an integral part of the composition as well as the device which 'fixes' objects in their proper place.

The background thus completed, I started underpainting the subject of the piece – the toad. A dark green (Prussian Blue and Yellow Ochre) was painted over the area of the toad and the edges were softened into the background with the smallest Dalon fan, rendering a silhouette. Into the soft paint I began to dot in the toad's top colour (Yellow Ochre, Titanium White and Terre Verte, to give a pale grey-green) and I used the actual shape and position of these spots of paint to describe the curves and lines of the toad's body. Paint a little, then stand back and study is the rule; slowly build up the detail, the light and shade, the atmosphere of the painting as you go. The time spent achieving an image in paint is what gives it its depth of feeling, so work carefully and build slowly towards the finish of your work.

The eyes – the colour first, the black pupils second, and the highlights last – usually come at the end of the job, yet with this particular painting one crucial stage remained: the bright shaft of light that would cut right through the composition. I left the picture to go off for a day, then began carefully overpainting the strip of bright illumination with bright gold (Titanium White and Chrome Yellow) on a D.77 No. 2. Every surface facing the light source was filled in and the contours were faithfully followed. When the toad was thus overpainted, I lightened the colour with more Titanium White to separate further and enhance this, the focal point of my piece. The worm was dealt with last of all, and it was not difficult to find a model out in the garden.

Finishing a picture is a wonderfully satisfying moment. Drop your (beautifully cleaned) brush into your brush pot and sit back. Try to be another person who looks on the work for the first time and give an honest appraisal. Seeing a steady improvement in your painting is well worthwhile, and each picture finished leads you on to the next; to another chance to do better.

Fig. 67 *The Toad and the Worm*

Contrast is a useful device in wildlife painting, where the nature of your subject can be seen in comparison with objects familiar to the viewer. Temperament, scale and texture can be underlined in this way, and in the picture of the brooding robin (**fig. 69**) the rusty metal oil-lamp and the coarse wooden planking give us clear information as to the bird's size and the softness of its plumage. The broom handle and the old fishing rod suggest some of the clutter in which a robin might well feel at home, and so inform us further as to the little bird's nature. The strong shaft of sunlight, just catching the nesting bird, apart from having a strong visual effect of its own, captures that special moment when the hitherto hidden bird is suddenly seen illuminated. The very static nature of the devices around the robin and the fact that it is painted as an integral part of the still life, suggest that, although the bird is aware of being observed, it remains frozen in its situation. It is worth noting here that all substances have a surface character which must be suggested in paint. Here I have tried to paint a living bird covered in feathers; but a porcelain figure of a robin, however realistic, would still be made of porcelain and must therefore appear so in your picture.

Fig. 68

Fig. 69 *Robin*

The composition of the hedgehogs (**fig. 70**) was considered after I had seen a baby hedgehog's face and realized, first, that I had not really seen a hedgehog's face in detail before (they are usually tucked out of sight) and, second, what a delightful face it was. I used a setting of smooth roots and autumn leaves to give contrast and scale, and painted three of the creatures to give three slightly differing aspects of the face. The spines were achieved by painting the body shape in Vandyke Brown and then, using a Dalon No. 1 pencil brush, with a single stroke per spine, painting in the buff colour of the prickles into the wet oil paint.

Fig. 70 *Hedgehogs*

Do not waste time painting every perfect blade of grass unless it has a clear purpose in supporting the point of your picture. If you wish to express the wonderful diversity and brilliance of colour found in the bird world by painting a jay confronting a cock pheasant, you need no more than the merest suggestion of background, letting the riot of colour in the plumage be the sum total of the work. If, on the other hand, you wish to describe the delicacy and jewel-like quality of a tiny mouse, placing your subject against a great scaffolding of dark branches and leaves really emphasizes the exquisiteness of the mouse to your audience and makes a very clear statement of your intent. Here (**fig. 71**), the leaves also serve to hide the weasel and give it a menacing, lurking quality, further describing and contrasting the two subjects of the picture.

Fig. 71 *Weasel and Mouse*

Fig. 72 *Python and Prey*

A python with its prey (**fig. 72**) is a subject with a wealth of opportunities for the painter. The contours of a snake can be formed into an endless variety of shapes. They coil and intertwine, over and under, and are a wonderful visual maze for the viewer. Here I have set the snake on a sand background which suggests by colour the snake's integration with its environment. The pattern of the scales is a work of art in itself. Like a tapestry with each stitch a subtly different colour, the scales describe the beautiful forms of the creature beneath the skin. The head of the serpent is expressionless, alien, and the bird is all but lost beneath the massive power of the coils – just a hint of colour, already overwhelmed.

Using oil paint, I started with Vandyke Brown over the whole picture area and left this for three days to set dry. On this I painted with a Dalon 1 inch flat the sand colour, Yellow Ochre mixed with Zinc White, and stippled this with a Rowney bristle stippler to achieve an even colour, textured as sand. I drew in the outline of the snake with a 2H pencil and began painting in the illuminated areas of the snake's skin with the sand colour lightened with Titanium White. Each scale was achieved by a single stroke of a Dalon D.77 No. 1 brush. The shadows cast on to the sand were created by removing the overpainted sand colour to reveal the dark underpainting. This can be

done with a dry brush or a rag, or with anything that will give you a satisfying result. Where the snake disturbed the sand with its coils, I used a stiff brush (a Dalon D.44 is fairly unyielding) to re-create what had happened in life. The result can be uncannily accurate. The forms of the snake were shaded by painting on the same Vandyke Brown as the underpaint and then dotting in the scales in long, lateral lines along the forms of the body. I allowed the paint to blend naturally as I moved my brush from the wet, dark paint to the slightly drier pale colour. By this stage I was using small brushes and working on very small areas. I reinforced light against dark and rough against smooth to keep all the essential forms within the piece readable and clear.

The feathers were painted with a very rough old brush (something like a No. 4) and I deliberately left the brush to give me a ruffled effect. I painted the shadows on the plumage first and then the highlights over the top. Pure Titanium White highlights to bring the serpent to life and Lamp Black with Vandyke Brown to reinforce the deepest shadow concluded the picture. After a day I softened some parts of the work with a fan. You, too, will get into the habit of looking at what you do with the overall effect in mind, changing and adapting where you feel improvement can be made as you go along.

128